Quick Cuisine

By Terry Fraser

© Terry Fraser, 1984
LIBERTY PUBLISHING COMPANY
Cockeysville, Maryland

All Rights Reserved. This publication may not be reproduced in whole or in part by any means without prior written consent.

Published by:

Liberty Publishing Company, Inc.
50 Scott Adam Road
Cockeysville, Maryland 21030

Library of Congress #83-82661
ISBN 0-89709-130-2

Manufactured USA

For Bob
and our
ever-hungry offspring

Table of Contents

	Page
Foreword	1
Basic Kitchen Supplies	2
Appetizers, Soups and Breads	3
Salads and Dressings	21
Vegetables and Side Dishes	37
Chicken, Fish and Cheese Dishes	49
Beef, Lamb, Pork and Veal	71
Desserts	91
Glossary	121
Appendix	127
Index	133

Author's Foreword

The recipes that follow are our family favorites, used by me during years as a "single" businessperson/homemaker and later as a wife and parent. My three children, now in their early twenties, participated in active competition in swimming, badminton, regional tennis and Little League baseball. As a result, the family was always on the go, with healthy appetites. This gave me limited time to spend in the kitchen.

Now that the younger members of our family are on their own, they have asked to have copies of many of these recipes, for the same reasons I needed them. And, as co-owner and operator of a party supply retail shop, I still find time to be a scarce commodity. During the work week, I fall back on these "quickies" that average 15 minutes preparation time.

For best results, the reader should do the following:

1. Read the *complete* recipe *before* starting preparation.
2. Check kitchen supplies for all ingredients and correct size pans.
3. Purchase any necessary ingredients, preferably of best quality.
4. Assemble all ingredients and pans.
5. Re-read the recipe and preheat oven (10–15 minutes) when necessary.

Eternal thanks to my spouse and children who endured legions of "test" recipes and to the many family members and friends who shared their favorites.

Basic Kitchen Supplies

Potato Peeler
Sharp Paring Knife
Sharp Carving Knife
Serrated Bread Knife
Grater
Wooden Spoon
Cookie Sheet and/or Jelly Roll Pan
Measuring Spoons
Measuring Cup
Can Opener—Manual and/or Electric
Strainer
Sifter (possible alternative, use strainer)
Cutting Board
Rolling Pin (in a pinch, use cola or wine bottle)
Spatula (Teflon, if your pans are Teflon-coated)
Soup Scoop
Wire Whisk
Pastry Brush
Slotted Spoon
Tongs
Corkscrew

Colander
Salad Spinner
Garlic Press
Juice Squeezer
Rubber Scraper
Cake/Pie Cooling Rack
Tea Kettle
Mixing Bowls—3 different sizes
Frying Pans—10 inch skillet and a smaller one
Oven Casserole Dishes (pyrex)—1-1/2 qt., larger
Baking Pans—7" × 11", 8" × 8", 9" × 13" × 2", 9" pie pan, 2 round cake pans, tube pan, spring release pan, 9" × 5" × 3" loaf pan, 15-1/2 × 10-1/2
Pepper Mill
Toaster
Saucepans with covers—1-1/2 qt., 2 qt., double boiler, 5 qt.
Muffin Tin
Electric Hand Mixer
Electric Blender or Food Processor

Appetizers, Soups and Breads

Included in this section are a number of spreads and dips, along with a suggestion for the crackers to be served with most of them. We have discovered that certain crackers complement various spreads far better than others. There are, of course, many terrific crackers on the market. Following are a few of the brands that we have particularly enjoyed and some of the items we served with them:

Bremner Wafers (Brie Cheese)
Carrs Biscuits (Cheddar Cheese)
Corn Diggers (Spinach Dip)
Crocottes (Boursin Cheese, Brie Cheese)
Euphrates Sesame Seed (Crab ring)
Lahvosh (great with Brie, Boursin, spreadable cheeses)
Kavli (Cheddar Cheese, King Christian Cheese)
Ritz (Cheddar, Port Wine Cheese)
Triscuit ("Jezebel")
Wasa Hearty Rye (Corned Beef Spread)

Melons make wonderful, quick to prepare, first or last courses for a meal. The secret is, of course, to select a ripe one.

Cantaloupe:

If picked fully mature, it will have some rough fibers on the stem end. Melon is oval-shaped, with rough cream-colored raised netting. The netting should cover the entire surface, any smooth spot is a bad sign. The skin underneath may be greenish, beige or golden yellow. A *golden yellow* means the melon is ready to eat *right away*. If other colors dominate, let the melon ripen at room temperature before chilling.

Honeydew:

A slight give to the rind shows ripeness, and it should be *creamy white* or *creamy yellow* color. Rind that is dead white or has a greenish tinge shows the melon was picked too soon. A good one will feel *soft* and *velvety*, and *slightly sticky* or *oily*. If it

Appetizers, Soups and Breads

feels hard and is shiny, it was picked too soon.

Watermelon:

The huge melons yield the most fruit to rind. *Avoid* a shiny looking rind and a greenish or dead white spot where it rested on the ground. Instead, it *should have* a somewhat velvety bloom on the rind and a slightly yellowish or amber colored ground spot. Also, *avoid* those with a white streak running the length of the melon. If melon is cut, look for firm red flesh and black or dark brown seeds. *Reject* melons with soft, white immature seeds or melons with seeds that have broken away from their cavities or have a sugary look around the seeds.

Crenshaw:

Large melon with a flattened or rounded end and rather pointed stem end. The skin is smooth with slight lengthwise ribbing and no netting. When ripe, the skin is a beautiful gold.

Persian:

Resembles an oversized cantaloupe, however, it is somewhat rounder and has finer, flatter netting. The *sign* of *immaturity* here is netting of a dark or greenish-black color.

In the main, avoid all melons that are soft, as opposed to melons that give gently. Soft melons are overripe. Any melon that "sloshes" when shaken will be musky inside and may have started to sour. Discard any with a soft and wet stem end because they have already started to decay.

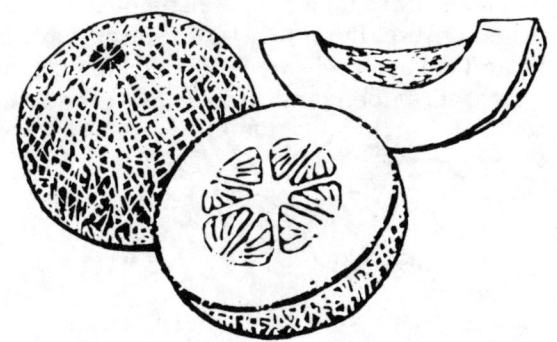

Artichoke Spread

Preparation time: 10 minutes

Cooking time: 30 minutes

Serves: 8–10 (3-1/2 cups)

1 jar (11-1/2 oz.) *artichokes in water*
1 cup *finely chopped onions* (*or less, if desired*)
1 cup *mayonnaise*
1 cup *Parmesan cheese*

Drain water from artichokes and chop them into small pieces. Mix together with onions, mayonnaise and cheese. Put into a 1-1/2 quart pyrex casserole and bake in preheated 350° oven for 30 minutes, or until bubbly and brown. Serve hot with crackers.

Baked Brie Pie

Preparation time: 10 minutes

Cooking time: (pastry) 12 minutes
(full pie) 25–30 minutes

Serves: 6 full or 12 appetizer servings

pastry for 9" pie—Pillsbury All-Ready Pie Crust
8 oz. *ripe Brie cheese*—rind removed
8 oz. *cream cheese, softened*
1/4 cup (1/2 stick) *butter, softened*
6 tablespoons *heavy cream*
4 *eggs, beaten*
4 dashes *red pepper* (*Tabasco sauce*)
1 tablespoon *chopped chives* (*frozen or in jar*)

Spread pastry in a *spring form* baking pan on bottom and about one inch up side of pan. Prick with a fork all over bottom of pastry. Bake in preheated 400° oven for 12 minutes.

Cream all other ingredients together. Mix well. Turn heat down to 375°. Pour mixture into baked crust and place into upper third of oven.

Bake 25–30 minutes until puffed and lightly browned. Remove from oven and let stand for 5 minutes. Remove sides of pan.

Serve hot (best) or cold.

Bleu Cheese Bites

Preparation time: 10 minutes

Cooking time: 12 to 15 minutes

Serves: 10–20 (40 "bites")

1 package refrigerated biscuits (10 biscuits)
4 tablespoons butter or margarine
4 tablespoons crumbled bleu cheese

Quarter biscuits; arrange in two 8" × 1-1/2" round baking dishes with a little space between them. In saucepan, melt together butter or margarine and the bleu cheese; drizzle over biscuits. Bake in preheated 400° oven for 12 to 15 minutes or until browned.

Bob's Favorite Corned Beef Spread

Preparation time: 5 minutes

Cooking time: 0

Serves: 6–8

1/2 (12 oz.) can corned beef
1 (8 oz.) package cream cheese, softened
1 to 2 tablespoons prepared horseradish—or more to taste

Flake 1/2 can of corned beef. Mix thoroughly together with softened cream cheese. Add 1 to 2 tablespoons horseradish and mash all together with a fork. Serve with Wasa Hearty Rye Crackers.

Cheese Ball

Preparation time: 10 minutes

Cooking time: 0

Freezing Time: 1 hour

Serves: 10–12

1 package (8 oz.) cream cheese, softened
1 package (8 oz.) Wispride cheese with port wine, softened
1 package (4 oz.) bleu cheese, softened
1 small onion (1/4 cup) finely chopped or grated
2 tablespoons Worcestershire sauce
crushed walnuts or pecans
chopped parsley

Blend all ingredients except nuts and parsley together with a fork. Form into one large or two small balls. Put in freezer for about 1 hour. Remove from freezer and roll cheeseball in chopped parsley and crushed nuts. Serve with crackers.

Cheese Puffs

Preparation time: 10 minutes

Cooking time: 1–2 minutes

Serves: 10–20 (40 puffs)

2 cups mayonnaise
1/2 cup finely grated Parmesan cheese (freshly grated, if possible; otherwise packaged)
2 tablespoons finely grated onion
2 teaspoons prepared hot mustard
40 Melba Toast rounds

Mix together all ingredients (through mustard). Spread on Melba Toast rounds—use 1 heaping teaspoon per round. Broil 6 inches from heat (preheated oven) for 1–2 minutes.

Chutney Appetizer Spread

Preparation time: 5 minutes

Cooking time: 0

Serves: 8–10 (35 appetizers)

1 8 oz. package cream cheese
1 (1 lb. 4 oz.) can crushed pineapple, drained
1 (8 oz.) jar chutney (Sun Brand "Major Gray's Chutney")
sesame crackers

    Place cream cheese on serving plate. Blend pineapple and chutney; spoon over cream cheese. Surround with crackers to serve.

Crab Ring Appetizer

Preparation time: 10 minutes

Cooking time: 0

Serves: 8–10

3 (8 oz. each) packages cream cheese, softened
1 pound back fin crabmeat, fresh or canned
1 cup catsup or chili sauce
1 tablespoon (or more, to taste) prepared horseradish

    Remove any shells from crabmeat. Shape cream cheese into a ring and press crabmeat to coat ring. Place on a serving dish.
    Mix together 1 cup of catsup or chili sauce with 1 tablespoon (or to taste) of horseradish. Place catsup mixture in center of ring. Serve with Euphrates Sesame Seed Crackers.

Hot Jezebel

Preparation time: 5 minutes

Cooking time: 0

Serves: 10–12 (2-1/4 cups)

2 cups apricot-pineapple preserves (if combo preserves aren't available, use 1 cup of apricot and 1 cup pineapple).
1/4 cup prepared horseradish
3 teaspoons dry mustard
1 teaspoon freshly ground black pepper
cream cheese
crackers

Mix together preserves, horseradish, dry mustard and ground black pepper. Store in a covered jar in refrigerator. To serve, place an 8-ounce brick of cream cheese on a serving platter and top with about 1/3 cup of hot Jezebel. Serve with crackers.

Mystery Meatballs

Preparation time: 15 minutes

Cooking time: 1 hour

Serves: 6–8 (approximately 24 meatballs)

1-1/2 cup quick cooking oats
3 large eggs, beaten
1 package dry onion soup mix (1 envelope)
3 lbs. ground beef
salt and pepper to taste

Sauce:

1 12 oz. bottle chili sauce
1-1/3 cups water
1/2 cup brown sugar
1 16 oz. can sauerkraut
1 16 oz. can jellied cranberry sauce

Add oatmeal, eggs and dry soup mix to hamburger. Mix well. Shape into balls. Place in 9" × 13" baking pan. Combine sauce ingredients in sauce-

Appetizers, Soups and Breads

pan and simmer until cranberry sauce melts. Spoon over meatballs and bake in preheated 350° oven for one hour or until done.

Nachos

Preparation time: 10 minutes

Cooking time: 6 minutes

Serves: 4–6

1 (7 oz.) *bag tortilla chips*
1 (16 oz.) *can refried beans*
1 *cup cheddar cheese, shredded*
1 *can (3 oz.) green chilies, chopped*
8 *oz. commercial sour cream (optional)*

Layer tortilla chips in flat baking pan. Spread refried beans on chips. Sprinkle cheese on top, followed by chilies. Heat in preheated 350° oven 6 minutes or until cheese melts. Top with sour cream, if desired. If you prefer a "hotter" taste, add chili powder to taste before baking.

Nantucket Special

Preparation time: 10 minutes

Cooking time: 40 minutes

Serves: 10–12 (2-1/2 cups)

2 (5 oz. each) *jars Old English cheese spread*
2 (5 oz. each) *jars garlic cheese spread*
4 *large scallions, chopped (tops and bottoms)*
1 *clove garlic, minced*
1 (7 oz.) *jar minced clams plus 1/2 jar of liquid*
big dash of Worcestershire sauce
1/4 *cup green pepper, minced*

Combine all ingredients in 1 quart baking dish and bake in preheated 350° oven for approximately 40 minutes. Allow to stand for 10 minutes before serving.

Serve with chips for dipping.

Shrimp Mold I

Preparation time: 10 minutes

Cooking time: 3 minutes

Chilling Time: overnight or at least 5 hours

Serves: 12–14

1 can tomato soup, undiluted
1 (8 oz.) package cream cheese, softened
1 envelope Knox unflavored gelatin
1/2 cup cold water
1/2 teaspoon salt
1/4 cup celery, chopped
1 cup green onions (and tops) chopped
1 pound small cooked shrimp

    Soak gelatin in 1/2 cup cold water for 5 minutes. Heat undiluted tomato soup to boiling. Add gelatin and remaining ingredients and mix well. Pour into a 1 quart mold that has been lightly greased with mayonnaise. Chill at least 5 hours or overnight. Unmold and serve with crackers.

Shrimp Mold II

Preparation time: 10 minutes

Cooking time: 2 minutes (boil water)

Refrigeration time: 1 hour plus several hours more (or overnight)

Serves: 6–8

1 (3 oz.) package lemon jello
1 cup boiling water
3/4 cup chili sauce
2 tablespoons vinegar
1 teaspoon Worcestershire sauce
dash of Tabasco sauce
2 tablespoons horseradish
2 cups canned shrimp (washed by running cold water over them)

    Mix jello and boiling water. Refrigerate. When partially set (about an hour), add remaining ingredients and pour into mold. Refrigerate for several hours or overnight. Serve with crackers.

Spinach Dip

Preparation time: 10 minutes

Cooking time: egg (hard-boiled) 15 minutes

Chilling time: at least one hour

Serves: 4

1 package (10 oz.) frozen chopped spinach—defrosted and drained well
2 hard-cooked eggs
3 large scallions
1/8 cup lemon juice (or more to taste)
1/4 cup mayonnaise
salt and pepper to taste

Drain thawed uncooked spinach thoroughly (squeeze out with your hands until as dry as possible). Chop scallions fine; also chop the hard-cooked eggs. Mix all the ingredients together. Refrigerate for at least an hour. Serve with Nabisco Cornettes or Corn Diggers or other crisp corn crackers.

Alternate serving suggestion: cut center out of unsliced loaf of pumpernickel or rye bread, and make small dipping pieces out of removed bread. Place spinach mixture into cavity of loaf, with small pieces around serving dish.

Spinach Dip in Cabbage

Preparation time: 15 minutes

Cooking time: 10 minutes (spinach)

Serves: 20 to 24 (6 cups)

3 (10 oz.) *packages frozen chopped spinach*
1 *cup chopped green onion*
1 (16 oz.) *carton commercial sour cream*
2 *cups mayonnaise*
2 *teaspoons herb-seasoned salt*
1 *teaspoon dried whole dillweed*
1-1/2 *teaspoon dried whole oregano*
juice of 1 lemon
1 *large red cabbage*

Cook spinach according to package directions; drain well and stir in next 7 ingredients. Chill. Trim core end of cabbage to form a flat base. Cut a crosswise slice from the top, making it wide enough to remove about a fourth of the head; then lift out enough inner leaves from the cabbage to form a shell about 1 inch thick. (Reserve slice and inner leaves of cabbage for use in another recipe).

Spoon dip into cavity of cabbage and serve with an assortment of fresh vegetables.

Vegetables (any or all)
Cherry tomatoes, raw cauliflower, raw carrots, raw celery, radishes, scallions, cucumbers, green peppers.

Triscuit Topper

Preparation time: 15 minutes

Cooking time: approximately 3 minutes

Serves: 12–16 (3-1/2 cups)

1-1/2 *cups shredded sharp cheddar cheese*
1 *cup ripe olives, chopped*
1/2 *cup onion, chopped*
1/2 *cup mayonnaise*
1 *teaspoon curry powder* (or more, if desired)

Mix all together. Store in refrigerator in a glass jar. When ready to serve, spread mixture on triscuits (or melba toast) and put under preheated broiler until bubbly (approximately 3 minutes). Mixture will keep in refrigerator for a month.

Corn and Tuna Bisque

Preparation time: 15 minutes

Cooking time: same as preparation time

Serves: 3–5 (5 cups)

2-1/2 tablespoons butter
2-1/2 tablespoons flour
3 cups milk
1-1/2 chicken bouillon cubes
1 (16 oz.) can of whole kernel golden corn
1 (7 oz.) can of tuna, drained & shredded
salt and pepper to taste
approximately 2 teaspoons of curry powder, or
 approximately 2 tablespoons of sherry

In the top of a double boiler, melt the butter and add the flour. Cook, stirring constantly, until blended. Add the milk and the bouillon cubes and stir until thick.

Stir in the corn and its liquid. When hot, add the shredded tuna. Heat through. Season to taste with *either* curry powder *or* dry sherry, and salt and pepper.

Crabmeat Bisque

Preparation time: 5 minutes

Cooking time: 10 minutes

Serves: 4

1 can pea soup
1 can tomato soup
2 soup cans of milk
1/2 cup cooking sherry
1 pound claw crabmeat

Remove any shells from crabmeat. Combine all ingredients. Cook over low flame until mixture simmers. Let simmer for about 5 minutes. Serve hot.
Serve with French bread and tossed salad.

Curried Pea Soup

Preparation time: 5 minutes

Cooking time: 10 minutes

Serves: 6

1 box frozen green peas
1 medium sliced onion (3/4 cup)
1 carrot
1 stalk sliced celery
1 sliced potato
1 clove garlic
1 teaspoon salt
1 scant teaspoon curry powder
2 cans chicken stock
1 cup heavy cream

Place vegetables, seasonings and one can stock in saucepan and bring to boil. Cover and simmer 15 minutes. Transfer to electric blender. Cover and turn motor on high, then remove cover so that remaining stock and cream can be poured in. Serve hot or cold and garnish with a spoonful of sour cream and fresh dill. Soup can be frozen *without* cream in it.

Jenny's Favorite Crab Soup

Preparation time: 10 minutes

Cooking time: 1 hour

Serves: 18–20

5 cans (10-1/2 oz. each) vegetable-beef soup, undiluted
1 pound claw crab meat, fresh or canned
1 can (17 oz.) peas
1 can (16 oz.) string beans
1 can (6 oz.) tomato paste
1 can (17 oz.) golden whole kernel corn
1 teaspoon McCormick Seafood Seasoning
2 soup cans water
salt & pepper to taste

Add everything together in a large pot. Use cans just as they are (do *not* dilute or drain). Simmer for one hour, stirring occasionally. Can be frozen.

Aloha Muffins

Preparation time: 10 minutes

Cooking time: 12–15 minutes

Serves: 12 muffins

2 cups biscuit (Bisquick) mix
2 tablespoons granulated sugar
1/2 teaspoon baking soda
1/4 cup flaked coconut
2 tablespoons cooking oil
1 large egg
1 (8 oz.) container pineapple yogurt

Using a fork, combine Bisquick mix with sugar, coconut and baking soda. Add rest of ingredients and stir just until all of the dry ingredients are moistened. Fill greased muffin tin cups two-thirds full. Bake in preheated 400° oven for 12 to 15 minutes or until golden brown.

These muffins are not too sweet, are especially good with ham dinner, and are best served hot.

Cheese Bread

Preparation time: 10 minutes

Cooking time: 2–5 minutes

Serves: 6

1 stick butter or margarine
1/3 cup grated Romano cheese
1/4 cup grated Parmesan cheese
1 teaspoon paprika
12 oz. mozzarella cheese, sliced
garlic salt—a light sprinkle
1 loaf French bread, cut into halves lengthwise

Preheat broiler of oven. Melt butter, let cool. Add Romano and Parmesan cheese and paprika. Stir to blend but not to let cheese melt. Place mozzarella slices on cut sides of one loaf French bread, halved lengthwise. Spread with butter mixture. Sprinkle with garlic salt. Broil two to five minutes until lightly browned.

Appetizers, Soups and Breads

Cornbread

Preparation time: 15 minutes

Cooking time: 20 minutes

Serves: 12 (2 slices each)

Yield: about 24 squares

2-1/4 cup yellow cornbread mix
3 tablespoons granulated sugar
1/2 cup vegetable oil
3 eggs, beaten
1 (8-1/2 oz.) can cream-style corn
1-1/2 cup (6 oz.) shredded Longhorn cheese
1 large onion, grated (3/4 cup)
2 large canned jalapeño peppers, seeded and chopped

Combine all, mixing well. Heat a well-greased 13" × 9" × 2" pan in 400° oven for 3 minutes. Pour batter into hot pan and bake at 450° for 20 minutes or until cornbread is golden brown. Cut into 2-inch squares.

Easy Beer Bread

Preparation time: 5 minutes

Cooking time: 1 hour

Serves: 6–8 slices

3 cups self-rising flour
3 tablespoons granulated sugar
12 oz. (1 can) warm beer

Preheat oven to 375°. Into a mixing bowl, put flour and sugar, then add warm beer. Stir to blend together. Spoon into a greased 9" × 5" × 3" loaf pan. Bake for 1 hour. Serve hot (best) or at room temperature, or can be toasted. Can be varied by adding either onion flakes or cheese or cinnamon to taste.

Garlic Bread

Preparation time: 10 minutes
Cooking time: approximately 7 minutes
Serves: 6

1 stick butter or margarine (1/2 cup)
vegetable oil
Parmesan cheese
garlic salt
oregano
French bread

Slice bread into 1/2-inch thick slices. Spread a little vegetable oil with a pastry brush over each slice. Then, with a knife, spread butter or margarine over each slice. Sprinkle bread with lots of Parmesan cheese, a medium amount of garlic salt, and a little oregano. Place on a cookie sheet. Bake in preheated 400° oven for 7 minutes or until light brown.

Zucchini Bread

Preparation time: 10 minutes
Cooking time: 50–55 minutes
Serves: 6–8

2 cups Bisquick
1-1/2 cups pared and shredded zucchini
3/4 cup granulated sugar
1/4 cup vegetable oil
3 large eggs
1 teaspoon vanilla
2 teaspoons ground cinnamon
1 teaspoon ground nutmeg
1/2 cup chopped nuts

Heat oven to 350°. Grease bottom *only* of loaf pan (9″ × 5″ × 3″). Beat all ingredients on low speed, scraping bowl constantly, 30 seconds. Beat on medium speed, scraping bowl occasionally, 1 minute. Pour into pan. Bake in 350° oven until wooden toothpick inserted comes out clean, 50 to 55 minutes. Cool 10 minutes; remove from pan. Cool before slicing. Store in refrigerator.

Salads and Dressings

Salad Tips

Chopping vs. tearing:
When preparing your salad in advance, tear lettuce. This way, the edges won't darken as quickly.
When planning to serve the salad right away, go ahead and chop. It's a quick, easy way to a crisp salad.
Wash greens in cold water early in the day you are going to serve them. Spin dry in a salad spinner. Place spinner in refrigerator until just before your meal. Your greens will be really crisp when you are ready to serve them.
Use freshly ground pepper in recipes. (Buy a pepper mill.)

Apple-Bacon Salad

Preparation time: 15 minutes

Cooking time: 0 (Put garlic in oil overnight)

Serves: 6

1/2 pound bacon
1 head iceberg lettuce
3 red apples
2/3 cup garlic oil (place 2–3 peeled garlic cloves in oil, let stand overnight)
2 teaspoons lemon juice
1/2 cup Parmesan cheese
1 bunch scallions, sliced
1 cup croutons
1/2 teaspoon freshly ground pepper
1/4 teaspoon salt
1 egg, unbeaten

Cook bacon, until crisp, drain on absorbent paper and break into small pieces. Cut lettuce into bite-sized pieces. Quarter and core apples, but do not peel. Cut apples into thin slices and drop into garlic oil. Stir in lemon juice. Combine all ingredients in salad bowl. Toss until all traces of egg disappear. Serve at once.

Caesar Salad

Preparation time: 10 minutes

Cooking time: 0

Serves: 4 to 6

1 large head Romaine lettuce
1 egg yolk
1 teaspoon Dijon mustard
3 tablespoons Progresso olive oil
dash of Worcestershire sauce
1 anchovy filet
1 garlic clove, peeled
grated Parmesan cheese
seasoned croutons
dash of salt
dash of pepper
juice of 1 lemon

Rub wooden bowl with a garlic clove and sprinkle with salt. Tear head Romaine lettuce and sprinkle with grated Parmesan cheese and seasoned croutons. In a small bowl, mix together dash of salt, pepper and teaspoon Dijon mustard. Add 3 tablespoons Progresso olive oil and the juice of the lemon. Beat in egg yolk. Add a dash of Worcestershire sauce. Mash in anchovy filet. Toss over salad.

Cranberry-Pineapple Salad Mold
(great with turkey)

Preparation time: 25 minutes

Cooking time: 5 minutes

Refrigeration time: 1 hour plus 3 hours (or overnight)

Serves: 16

1 envelope unflavored gelatin
2 cups water plus 3 cups water
1 (6 oz.) package cherry flavor gelatin
1 (6 oz.) package lemon or lime flavor gelatin
1 (12 oz.) package fresh cranberries, coarsely chopped
2 medium celery stalks (3/4 cup)
1 (15-1/4 to 20 oz.) can pineapple chunks
1 cup granulated sugar

In 4-quart saucepan, evenly sprinkle unflavored gelatin over 2 cups water; cook over medium heat until gelatin is completely dissolved, stirring frequently. Remove saucepan from heat; stir in cherry flavor and lemon flavor gelatin until gelatin is completely dissolved. Stir in 3 cups cold water. Refrigerate until mixture thickens slightly, about one hour. Meanwhile, coarsely chop cranberries and mince celery; place in medium bowl. Drain pineapple; add chunks to cranberries with sugar, stirring until sugar is completely dissolved.

Fold fruit mixture into thickened gelatin. Pour into 12-cup Bundt pan or mold. Cover and refrigerate at least 3 hours.

Curried Tuna and Apple Salad

Preparation time: 15 minutes

Cooking time: 0

Serves: 6

3 cans (7 oz. each) white albacore tuna, drained
1 cup chopped celery
1/4 cup minced onion

Salads and Dressings

1 cup mayonnaise
1 apple—cored and chopped (*leave peel on*)
1 teaspoon curry powder
1/2 cup sour cream
1 tablespoon lemon juice
1/4 cup slivered almonds, *optional*

   Put tuna into a large bowl. Add 1 cup of chopped celery and one apple that has been cored and chopped. To all, add 1/4 cup minced (finely chopped) onion and 1 cup of mayonnaise. Stir in sour cream, curry powder and lemon juice. Serve on lettuce. Perhaps surround each serving with cherry tomatoes (4). Sprinkle nuts over salad.

Drew's Favorite Bleu Cheese Salad

Preparation time: 10 minutes

Cooking time: None, but lettuce should be chilled *at least* 2 hours

Serves: 5–6

1 medium head iceberg lettuce
6 oz. bleu cheese
1 medium to large sweet onion (red or Bermuda)—about 3/4 to 1 cup
9 tablespoons oil (peanut or Wesson)
3 tablespoons wine vinegar
1 level teaspoon sugar
1/2 teaspoon or more salt
freshly ground pepper—lots

   Wash, spin dry and chill lettuce. Chop into bite-sized pieces. Chop onion and add to lettuce in a large salad bowl. Crumble and add cheese. Sprinkle sugar, salt and pepper over all. *Toss with oil and vinegar. Add more oil and vinegar, if necessary, depending on size of head of lettuce. (3 parts oil to 1 part vinegar).

*Do not put oil and vinegar on this salad until just before you are ready to serve it.

Forgotten 4-Layer Salad

Preparation time: 15 minutes; also, thaw dessert topping

Cooking time: 0

Serves: 8

Salad

1 medium head lettuce, torn (about 6 cups)
1 small red onion, thinly sliced
2 cups thinly sliced cauliflowerets
2 medium zucchini (unpeeled) cut into thin slices (2 cups)

Horseradish Dressing

1/3 cup mayonnaise
1 tablespoon lemon juice
1 teaspoon Worcestershire sauce
1/2 cup frozen whipped dessert topping (thawed)
1/2 cup French salad dressing
1 tablespoon prepared horseradish
4–6 drops hot pepper sauce

In a salad bowl, layer lettuce, onion, cauliflowerets, and zucchini. Spread horseradish dressing over the top.* Cover tightly with clear plastic wrap or foil and refrigerate 6 hours or overnight. Toss just before serving.

*To make dressing: Combine mayonnaise, french dressing, lemon juice, horseradish, Worcestershire, and hot pepper sauce. Fold in whipped topping.

Fraser Cranberry Salad

Preparation time: 15 minutes

Cooking time: 0

Freezing time: 2 hours or overnight

Serves: 8

2 packages (3 oz. each) cream cheese, softened
2 tablespoons granulated sugar
2 tablespoons mayonnaise
1 can (16 oz.) jellied cranberry sauce
1 cup crushed pineapple, drained

1/2 cup chopped pecans
1/2 cup heavy cream, whipped

Cream together cheese and sugar, stir in mayonnaise. Fold in cranberry sauce, pineapple, nuts and whipped cream. Turn into a 9" × 5" × 3" loaf pan. Freeze until firm (at least 2 hours). Remove from freezer at least 15 minutes before serving. Cut into slices. Serve on shredded lettuce.

Fresh Cauliflower Salad

Preparation time: 15 minutes

Chilling time: 2 hours

Serves: 8 to 10

4 cups sliced cauliflower flowerets (1 small head)
1/2 cup chopped green pepper
1/4 cup chopped onion
2/3 cup commercially prepared sour cream
3 tablespoons mayonnaise
1 teaspoon dry mustard
1 teaspoon granulated sugar
1 tablespoon snipped fresh dill or 1 teaspoon dried dillweed
2 dashes hot pepper sauce
2 medium tomatoes, chopped—be sure tomatoes are chilled before stirring them into salad
salt & pepper

In a large bowl, stir together the cauliflower, green pepper and onion. Combine the sour cream, mayonnaise, dry mustard, sugar, dill and hot pepper sauce. Season to taste with salt and pepper. Gently stir dressing into vegetable mixture. Cover and chill for several hours. Just before serving, carefully stir chilled tomatoes into salad.

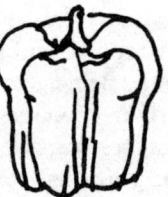

Frozen Coleslaw

Preparation time: 15 minutes

Freezing time: several hours or overnight

Serves: 8–10

1 *large head of cabbage, shredded (about 12 cups)*
1 *large green pepper, chopped*
1 *large carrot, shredded*
1 *teaspoon salt*
1 *cup vinegar*
1 *cup sugar*
1/4 *cup water*
1 *teaspoon dry mustard*
1 *teaspoon celery seed*

Combine vegetables, sprinkle with salt and let stand 1 hour. Drain mixture of any water that accumulates. (This is important.) Combine remaining ingredients in a saucepan. Bring to a boil; boil for 1 minute. Cool. Pour over cabbage mixture; stir well. Freeze in plastic freezer bags or containers in either single or multiple portions.

To serve, thaw in refrigerator at least 1 hour.

Frozen Salad

Preparation time: 10 minutes

Cooking time: 0

Freezing time: minimum of 2 hours or overnight

Serves: 12

2 *cups (16 oz.) commercially prepared sour cream*
2 *tablespoons lemon juice*
1/2 *cup granulated sugar*
1/8 *teaspoon salt*
1 *(8 oz.) can crushed pineapple (including liquid)*
1 *banana, diced*
1/4 *cup chopped pecans*
4 *drops red food coloring*
1 *can (16-1/2 oz.) pitted* bing cherries, *drained*
lettuce

Combine everything except lettuce. Spoon into large, fluted paper muffin cups in 3" muffin pans. Cover with plastic wrap and freeze. Remove from freezer at least 15 minutes before serving. Peel off paper and place salad on lettuce.

Salads and Dressings

Fruited Ham Salad

Preparation time: 15 minutes

Chilling time: 3–4 hours

Serves: 4

1 (15-1/4 oz.) can pineapple chunks in syrup
1/2 medium cantaloupe cut into balls or bite-sized chunks
1-1/4 pounds smoked cooked ham, cut into thin strips
1 banana, sliced
lettuce leaves
Pineapple Salad Dressing (see recipe)

Optional
1 avocado, sliced into bite-sized pieces (remove skin)

   Drain pineapple, reserving juice for dressing. Combine fruit and ham (except banana and optional-avocado). Toss gently. Chill 3–4 hours. A little before serving, add banana (otherwise it browns) and avocado slices. Mix gently. Spoon into a lettuce-lined bowl, and serve with Pineapple Salad Dressing that has been chilled.

Golden Rice Salad

Preparation time: 15 minutes

Cooking time: 20 minutes (rice)
       15 minutes (hard-boiled eggs)

Refrigerate: 2 hours or more

Serves: 8–10

1/4 cup salad oil
2 tablespoons vinegar
1-1/2 teaspoons salt
1/4 teaspoon freshly ground pepper
1 cup seedless ripe olives, cut in large pieces
2 hard-cooked eggs, diced
1-1/2 cup sliced celery
4-1/2 cups cooked rice (1-1/2 cup raw rice—cooked in 3 cups canned chicken broth)
1/4 cup chopped dill pickle
1 small onion, minced (1/4 cup)
2 tablespoons prepared Poupon mustard
1/2 cup mayonnaise
parsley & green onion tops

Cook rice in 3 cups canned chicken broth. Hard-boil 2 eggs. Blend together oil, vinegar, salt and pepper. Pour over hot cooked rice. Set aside to cool. Add all of the remaining ingredients. Top with fresh or dried parsley and chopped green onion tops if desired. Chill thoroughly.

Greek Salad

Preparation time: 20 minutes

Cooking time: 0

Serves: 10 to 12

2 large heads Romaine lettuce, washed & dried
1 bunch scallions, chopped
1 small red onion, thinly sliced
12 black olives
4 radishes, thinly sliced
1/2 cup crumbled feta cheese
1/4 teaspoon dried oregano
12 cherry tomatoes, cut in half
juice of 2 lemons
6–8 tablespoons olive oil

Salads and Dressings

Tear Romaine lettuce into bite-sized pieces. Combine lettuce with all ingredients except lemon juice and oil.*

Add lemon juice to salad and toss. Add olive oil, salt and pepper to taste and toss again. Serve at once.

If desired, prepare salad to this point several hours earlier and refrigerate. Add juice and oil just prior to serving.

Guacamole Salad

Preparation time: 10 minutes

Serves: 4

2 ripe* (soft) avocados
1 tablespoon lemon or lime juice
2 ripe tomatoes, finely chopped
1/2 cup green onions (scallions) thinly sliced
1/4 to 1/2 teaspoon garlic powder
Jane's Krazy Salt—to taste

Optional: 2 tablespoons green chilies, chopped

Cut avocados in half—lengthwise. Remove pits. Scoop avocado from shells and mash. Add lemon juice, tomatoes, scallions and garlic powder—blend. Season with salt to taste. Refill shells with mixture.

Ripe avocados feel quite soft. If they are still firm when purchased, let ripen at room temperature for 2 or 3 days.

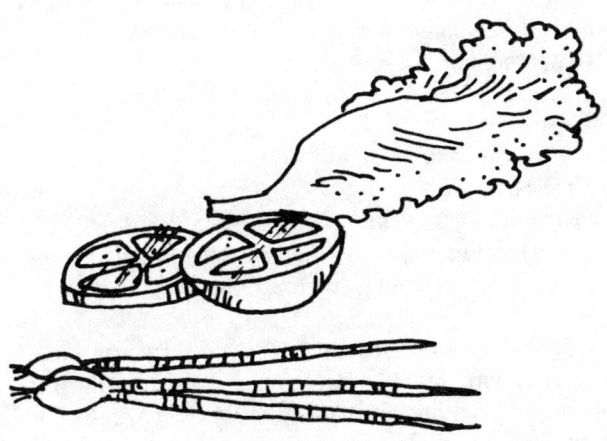

Ham and Melon Salad

Preparation time: 15 minutes

Cooking time: 2 hours or longer of chilling in refrigerator

Serves: 4

1 cup cooked chopped ham (one pre-cooked slice of ham)
6–8 teaspoons mayonnaise
1/4 cup chopped celery
1/4 cup sweet pickle relish, drained
1/4 cup raisins
1/8 teaspoon ground cloves
1/8 teaspoon salt
1 ripe honeydew, cut in quarters
1/4 cup mayonnaise, in addition to previous mayonnaise
1/4 cup lemon or orange/pineapple yogurt

    Combine ham with 6 tablespoons mayonnaise, celery, relish, raisins, cloves and salt; mix lightly. Fill melon halves with mixture. Cover, chill. Cut head melon in half; in half again. Serve with dressing of 1/4 cup mayonnaise and 1/4 cup yogurt, combined.

Ham-Rice Toss

Preparation time: 15 minutes

Cooking time: 20 minutes (rice)

Chilling time: 2 hours or more

Serves: 4

3 cups cooked regular rice, chilled (1/2 cup of uncooked rice)
1 cup cooked ham, diced
1/2 cup chopped green pepper
1 tablespoon minced onion
1/3 cup sliced celery
1/2 cup commercial Italian salad dressing
lettuce leaves
2 tomatoes, cut into wedges

    Combine first 6 ingredients, stirring well. Chill well. Serve on lettuce leaves and garnish with tomato wedges.

Hearty Ham Salad

Preparation time: 15 minutes

Chilling time: 2–3 hours

Serves: 6

3 cups cooked ham, diced
1-1/2 cups (6 oz.) sharp Cheddar cheese
2 cups diced apples (*unpeeled*)
1 cup diced celery
1/2 teaspoon lemon-pepper seasoning
3/4 to 1 cup mayonnaise
lettuce leaves

Combine all ingredients except lettuce; mix well. Chill 2 to 3 hours before serving. Serve on lettuce leaves.

Marinated Green Beans

Preparation time: 10 minutes

Cooking time: 20 minutes (for fresh beans)

Chilling time: 2 hours

Serves: 8

1/2 cup salad oil
1/2 cup wine vinegar
1 tablespoon fresh dill or 1 teaspoon dried dillweed
1/2 teaspoon dry mustard
1 clove garlic, minced
1/2 teaspoon granulated sugar
1/2 teaspoon salt
1/4 teaspoon freshly ground pepper
1 pound fresh green beans or 2 (10 oz. each) packages frozen cut beans, cooked
1/2 cut chopped onions

Wash beans; remove ends and strings. Cook whole beans, covered, in a small amount of boiling salted water for 20 minutes or until tender-crisp. Drain beans well. Mix together the salad oil, wine vinegar, dill, dry mustard, minced garlic, sugar, salt and pepper. Combine the cooked beans and onion. Pour marinade over vegetables. Cover and chill for several hours or overnight.

Waldorf Salad

Preparation time: 10 minutes
Cooking time: 0
Serves: 4–6

4 large eating apples
2 cups sliced celery
1/2 cup mayonnaise
1/4 cup sour cream
1/2 cup chopped English walnuts or pecans
salt and pepper to taste
salad greens

Core apples and chop (do not peel). Combine with celery in a large bowl. Add mayonnaise and sour cream, toss to coat evenly. Add salt and pepper to taste; toss in nuts. Line a salad bowl with salad greens; pile apple mixture into bowl and sprinkle with additional nuts, if you wish. Raisins or cut up dates may also be added, if desired.

Bleu Cheese Salad Dressing

Preparation time: 10 minutes
Chilling time: 2 hours
Serves: 10 (2-1/2 cups)

1 cup commercial sour cream
1 cup mayonnaise
1/4 cup red wine vinegar
3 oz. bleu cheese, crumbled
2 tablespoons chopped green onion
2 tablespoons chopped fresh parsley
1 teaspoon lemon juice

Combine all ingredients, stirring well. Chill for several hours before serving. Serve over salad greens. Store in refrigerator.

Salads and Dressings

Caesar Salad Dressing

Preparation time: 10 minutes

Chilling time: 2 hours

Serves: 12 (3-1/2 cups)

3 extra large eggs
1 stalk celery, coarsely chopped
1 (2 oz.) can anchovies, drained
2 cloves garlic
2 tablespoons prepared mustard
1 tablespoon lemon juice
1 teaspoon monosodium glutamate
1 teaspoon freshly ground pepper
1/2 teaspoon salt
2 cups vegetable oil

    Combine all ingredients, except oil, in container of electric blender, process until smooth. Add oil, 1/4 cup at a time, processing after each addition. Chill for several hours before serving. Serve dressing over salad greens. Store in refrigerator.

Celery Seed Salad Dressing

Preparation time: 10 minutes

Chilling time: 2 hours

Serves: 8 (2 cups)

1 cup vegetable oil
2/3 cup granulated sugar
1/4 cup tarragon wine vinegar
1/4 cup cider vinegar
3 tablespoons coarsely chopped onion
1 tablespoon paprika
1 tablespoon ground celery seeds
1-1/2 teaspoon salt
1/2 teaspoon dry mustard

    Combine all ingredients in container of electric blender; process mixture until smooth. Chill for several hours. Serve dressing over salad greens.

Italian Salad Dressing

Preparation time: 5 minutes

Cooking time: 15 minutes to hard-boil egg

Serves: 4 (1-1/3 cups)

1 clove garlic, peeled
1 hard-boiled egg, shelled
1/4 teaspoon granulated sugar
pinch of oregano
1 cup salad oil
1/3 cup red wine vinegar
salt and freshly ground pepper to taste
Parmesan cheese—1 teaspoon or more to taste

Crush garlic and egg. Combine with all other ingredients.

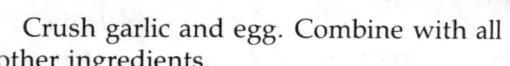

Pineapple Salad Dressing

Preparation time: 5 minutes

Cooking time: 5–10 minutes, chill at least several hours

Serves: 6 (1-1/2 cups)

1/2 cup granulated sugar
1 tablespoon all-purpose flour
reserved pineapple juice from 15-1/4 oz. can of chunks
1 egg, beaten
2 tablespoons vegetable oil
2 tablespoons lemon juice

Combine sugar and flour in a small saucepan. Add enough water to reserved pineapple juice to measure 3/4 cup. Add this and remaining ingredients to sugar mixture, mixing well. Cook over low heat, until thickened (about 5–10 minutes), stirring constantly. Chill thoroughly (at least 2 hours).

Serve over fruit salads or greens.

Vegetables and Side Dishes

Baked Tomatoes

Preparation time: 10 minutes

Cooking time: 15 minutes

Serves: 6

3 large tomatoes
vegetable oil
3/4 teaspoon salt
1/2 cup sharp Cheddar cheese
1/2 cup dry bread crumbs
1/4 cup (1/2 stick) butter or margarine, melted
3/4 teaspoon leaf basil, crumbled
1/8 teaspoon cayenne pepper

Wash tomatoes and cut in half; brush skin with oil. Place, cut side up, in an 8-cup shallow baking dish; sprinkle with salt.

Combine cheese, bread crumbs, melted butter or margarine, basil and cayenne pepper in a small bowl until well blended. Spoon a heaping tablespoon cheese mixture on top of each tomato half. Bake in preheated 350° oven for 15 minutes or until tomatoes are tender and topping is bubbly.

Broccoli Casserole

Preparation time: 15 minutes

Cooking time: 30–40 minutes

Serves: 6–8

2 packages frozen chopped broccoli cooked
1 can cream of mushroom soup, undiluted
1/2 cup mayonnaise
1 tablespoon lemon juice
1/2 cup grated Cheddar cheese
1 cup crushed cheese crackers

Drain cooked broccoli. Mix broccoli with soup. Add mayonnaise, lemon juice, and cheese. Put into 1-1/2 quart casserole (pyrex) and place 1 cup crushed cheese crackers on top. Bake in preheated 350° oven for 30 to 40 minutes, uncovered.

Broccoli/Cheese/Tomatoes

Preparation time: 15 minutes

Cooking time: 30 minutes

Serves: 6–8

2 (10 oz.) packages frozen broccoli
2 eggs, slightly beaten
1 (16 oz.) can stewed tomatoes
1 can Cheddar cheese soup (Campbell's)
Parmesan cheese
1/4–1/2 teaspoon oregano
parsley
dash of cumin
salt and pepper to taste

Cook broccoli according to directions on package and drain. Butter 7" × 11" pyrex casserole dish. Layer ingredients (broccoli, then tomatoes, then cheese soup, then eggs) in casserole. Sprinkle top with Parmesan cheese (lots) and parsley (lots), oregano and cumin, salt and pepper. Bake, uncovered for 30 minutes in a preheated 350° oven.

Continental Peas

Preparation time: 5 minutes

Cooking time: 7 minutes

Serves: 4

2 tablespoons butter or margarine
1 clove garlic, halved and peeled
1 teaspoon prepared mustard
1 teaspoon salt
1/4 cup water
2 cups frozen peas (from a 1 pound bag)

 Melt butter or margarine with garlic in a medium-sized saucepan; stir in mustard, salt, water and peas. Cover. Cook stirring several times for 5 minutes or just until peas are tender. Remove two garlic halves and discard.

Corn Pudding

Preparation time: 10 minutes

Cooking time: 1 hour, 10 minutes

Serves: 8

2 cans cream-style corn
5 eggs
*2 cups finely crushed puffed rice cereal
1/2 cup sugar
1/2 teaspoon salt
1 teaspoon vanilla
2 tablespoons flour
3/4 cup milk
1/2 pound melted butter

 Beat eggs, then mix in all other ingredients. Bake in 350° oven in large pyrex bowl 1 hour and 10 minutes.

* To crush cereal, either put in a blender or place between wax paper and roll with rolling pin or bottle on its side.

Creamy Corn Italiano

Preparation time: 10 minutes

Cooking time: 10–15 minutes

Serves: 4–6 (4-1/2 cups)

1/2 cup diagonally sliced green onions (scallions)
2 medium garlic cloves, minced
1/2 teaspoon basil leaves, crushed
1/2 teaspoon oregano
2 tablespoons butter or margarine
1 (10 oz.) can cream of celery soup
2 cans (16 oz. each) whole kernel golden corn, drained
1/4 cup milk
1/2 cup drained cut-up canned tomatoes

In saucepan, cook onions with minced garlic, oregano and basil in butter until tender. Add remaining ingredients. Heat, stir occasionally.

Oven Barbecued Corn

Preparation time: 5 minutes

Cooking time: 45 minutes

Serves: 4

1 cup catsup
1 small onion, chopped (1/4 cup)
2 tablespoons brown sugar
1 teaspoon dry mustard
1 teaspoon salt
3 cups frozen whole kernel corn (from 1-1/2 pound bag)
2 slices uncooked bacon, diced

Combine catsup, onion, brown sugar, dry mustard and salt in a 6-cup (1-1/2-quart) pyrex casserole. Add corn; mix thoroughly; top with diced bacon.

Bake uncovered in preheated 325° oven for 45 minutes or until corn is tender and bacon is crisp.

Eggplant Parmesan

Preparation time: 15 minutes

Cooking time: 20–25 minutes

Serves: 4–6

1 medium-sized eggplant (about 1-1/2 lbs.), pared and cut into 1/2-inch slices
1/4 cup grated Parmesan cheese
1/2 cup enriched cornmeal
1/2 cup butter or margarine, melted
1 can (8 ounces) pizza sauce
1 cup (4 ounces) shredded mozzarella cheese
2 tablespoons chopped parsley

Combine Parmesan cheese and cornmeal. Dip eggplant into butter; coat with cornmeal mixture. Place in a greased 15-1/2" × 10-1/2" jelly-roll pan (or cookie sheet). Spread slices with pizza sauce. Combine mozzarella cheese and parsley; sprinkle over pizza sauce. Bake in preheated 400° oven for 20 to 25 minutes or until eggplant is tender, and cheese is completely melted.

Green Bean Mushroom Combo

Preparation time: 5 to 10 minutes

Cooking time: 35 minutes

Serves: 6

2 (16 oz. each) cans french-style string beans, drained
or
2 packages (10 oz. each) frozen french-style string beans, cooked and drained
1 can (10-3/4 oz.) condensed cream of mushroom soup
1 teaspoon lemon juice
2 tablespoons chopped pimiento (optional)
1 can (3 oz.) french-fried onions

Combine beans (cooked and drained, if frozen), mushroom soup, lemon juice and chopped pimiento (optional). Turn into a one-quart casserole. Bake, uncovered, in preheated 350° oven for 30 minutes. Sprinkle with the french-fried onions. Continue baking, uncovered, 5 minutes longer.

Mediterranean Green Beans

Preparation time: 5 minutes

Cooking time: 25 minutes

Serves: 12

3 packages (10 oz. each) frozen french-cut string beans
1 can (16 oz.) whole tomatoes
1 can (10 oz.) tomato sauce
1 bottle (10 oz.) catsup
3 tablespoons brown sugar
1 tablespoon garlic powder or 1 clove garlic, crushed
3 bay leaves, coarsely crushed
butter to taste

Squeeze juice from the whole tomatoes and set aside for another use. Place the squeezed tomatoes and all other ingredients, except for butter, together in a saucepan and simmer for 25 minutes. Just before serving, add butter.

Herbed Potato Bake

Preparation time: 5 minutes

Cooking time: 1 hour

Serves: 3–4

1/3 cup melted margarine or butter
1/2 envelope onion soup mix
2 teaspoons rosemary
3 unpeeled baking potatoes

Combine 1/3 cup melted margarine or butter, 1/2 of envelope of onion soup mix and 2 teaspoons rosemary. Scrub potatoes, and cut into slices 1/2-inch thick. Combine margarine mixture and potatoes; toss gently. Arrange in rows in a shallow baking dish. *Cover* and bake in a preheated 350° oven for 1 hour.

Seasoned Onion Rice

Preparation time: 15 minutes

Cooking time: 1 hour

Serves: 6

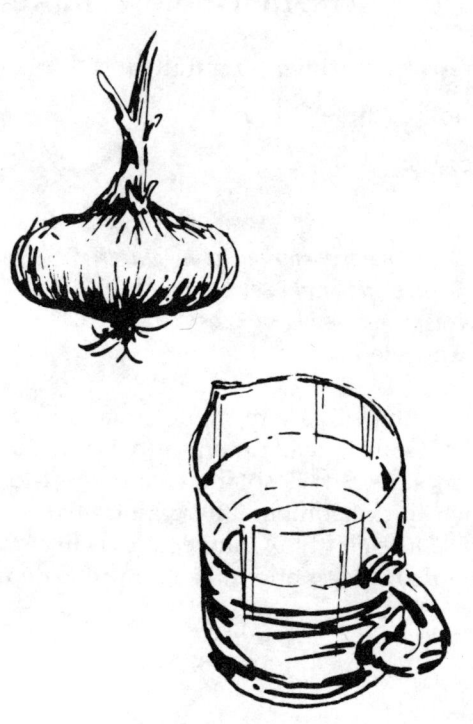

vegetable cooking spray
1 medium onion—finely chopped
1 cup uncooked regular rice
1 (10-3/4 oz.) can chicken broth, undiluted
3/4 cup water
1 tablespoon Worcestershire sauce
1 beef-flavored bouillon cube
1/4 teaspoon pepper

    Sauté onion 5 minutes, add remaining ingredients—bring to boil. Spray casserole with cooking spray. Add rice-onion mixture. Cover and bake at 350° (preheated oven) for 1 hour. (Use 1-1/2 qt. pyrex casserole.)

Irish Potato Casserole

Preparation time: 15 minutes

Refrigerate: overnight

Cooking time: 1 hour (30 minutes boiling and 30 minutes baking)

Serves: 8–10

8–10 medium potatoes, peeled and cut in half
1 (8 oz.) package cream cheese, softened
1 (8 oz.) carton commercial sour cream
1/2 cup butter or margarine, melted
1/4 cup chopped chives
1-1/2 teaspoons salt
paprika

    Cook potatoes in boiling water about 30 minutes or until tender. Drain potatoes and mash.
    Beat cream cheese with an electric mixer until smooth. Add potatoes and remaining ingredients except paprika; beat until just combined. Spoon mixture into a lightly buttered 2-quart pyrex casserole; sprinkle with paprika. Cover and refrigerate overnight.
    Remove from refrigerator 15 minutes before baking. Uncover and bake in 350° (preheated) oven for 30 minutes or until thoroughly heated.

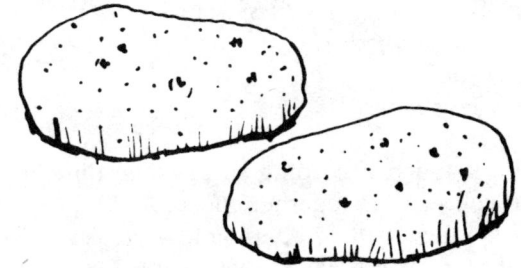

Spinach Casserole

Preparation time: 10 minutes

Cooking time: 25 minutes

Serves: 4

1 (3 oz.) *package cream cheese*
1/4 *pound butter or margarine*
1 *package frozen chopped spinach, cooked*
1 *can water chestnuts, sliced*
1 *small can artichoke hearts packed in water*
2 *teaspoons Parmesan cheese*
bread crumbs
salt & pepper to taste

    Cook spinach according to package directions. Drain well. Cream together cheese and butter and add to spinach. Salt and pepper to taste. Add sliced and drained water chestnuts to mixture. Line a 1-1/2 quart pyrex casserole dish with drained artichoke hearts. Put spinach mixture on top. Sprinkle bread crumbs and Parmesan cheese over spinach. Bake in preheated 325° oven about 25–30 minutes, until bubbly.

Texas Acorn Squash

Preparation time: 5 minutes

Cooking time: 45 minutes

Serves: 2

1 *acorn squash*
2 *tablespoons butter or margarine*
4 *tablespoons brown sugar*

    Cut squash in half, lengthwise. Remove seeds. Melt butter and sugar; spoon mixture into cavity of squash. Preheat oven to 375° and bake for 45 minutes or until squash is tender.

Baked Fruit with Sour Cream

Preparation time: 5 minutes

Cooking time: 35 minutes

Serves: 6–8

1 large can peach halves
1 can (16 oz.) apricot halves
1 can (16 oz.) pear halves
1 can (16-3/4 oz.) pitted bing cherries
2 boxes (10 oz. each) frozen strawberries, slightly thawed
1 cup dark brown sugar
1/4 cup fruit juice
1/2 cup rum
sour cream (commercial)

Drain first four fruits; save 1/4 cup juice. Arrange first four fruits in 13" × 9" × 2" pyrex casserole. Lay the contents of the boxes of frozen strawberries in the middle, side by side. Sprinkle fruits with brown sugar, add juice and rum. Bake in preheated 350° oven for 35 minutes. Serve warm, topped with sour cream.

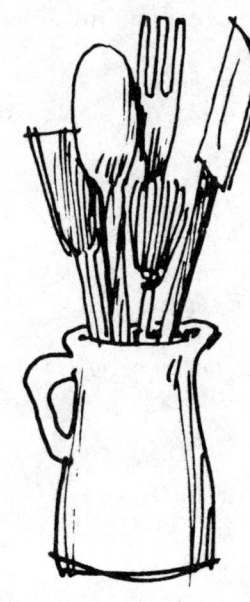

Hot Curried Fruit

Preparation time: 10 minutes
Cooking time: bake 30 minutes
Chilling time: overnight
Serves: 8–10

1 (16 oz.) can sliced pears
1 (16 oz.) can peach halves
1 (15-1/2 oz.) can pineapple chunks
1 (16 oz.) can apricot halves
1 (16 oz.) jar maraschino cherries
1 cup firmly packed brown sugar
1 tablespoon curry powder
1/4 cup butter or margarine
1/4 teaspoon ground cinnamon
1/8 teaspoon ground nutmeg
1/8 teaspoon salt
1 tablespoon lemon juice

Drain fruit and place in a 13" × 9" × 2" baking dish. Sprinkle with brown sugar and curry powder, and mix gently; dot with butter. Sprinkle with remaining ingredients. Refrigerate several hours or overnight.

Remove from refrigerator 15 minutes before baking. Bake in preheated 325° oven for 30 minutes.

Chicken, Fish and Cheese Dishes

Apricot Chicken

Preparation time: 5 minutes

Cooking time: 1 hour

Serves: 6

6 chicken breasts
1 package Lipton Onion Soup Mix
1 jar apricot preserves or marmalade (10 oz. jar)

   Line a 9" × 13" × 2" baking dish with foil. Dip breasts in soup mix. Spoon one heaping teaspoon of preserves on top of each breast. Bake uncovered at 350° for 1 hour or until chicken is done.

Baked Chicken Reuben

Preparation time: 5 minutes

Cooking time: 1-1/2 hours

Serves: 4

4 whole chicken breasts, halved and boned (these can be purchased "boned")
1/4 teaspoon salt
1/8 teaspoon pepper
1 (16 oz.) can sauerkraut, drained (press out excess liquid)
4 slices (about 4 × 6 each) natural Swiss cheese
1-1/4 cup bottled Thousand Island salad dressing
1 tablespoon chopped parsley

   Place chicken in greased baking pan. Sprinkle with salt and pepper. Place sauerkraut over chicken; top with swiss cheese. Pour dressing evenly over cheese. Cover with foil and bake in preheated 325° oven for about 1-1/2 hours or until fork can be inserted into chicken with ease. Sprinkle with chopped parsley before serving.

Baked Orange Chicken

Preparation time: 5 minutes

Cooking time: 1 hour

Serves: 8

2 broiler chickens, cut in parts or 8 large chicken breasts
1/2 cup water
1/2 cup orange juice
1/2 teaspoon garlic powder
1/2 teaspoon ground ginger
1 teaspoon honey
1 orange, sliced into round discs

Place chicken in 13" × 9" × 2" oven-proof casserole. Combine water, orange juice, garlic powder, ginger and honey; pour over chicken. Cover tightly with aluminum foil and bake in a preheated 350° oven for 1 hour, or until tender. Add orange slices about 10 minutes before chicken is done.

Chicken Breasts with Grapes

Preparation time: 5 minutes

Cooking time: 1 hour

Serves: 4

4 chicken breasts
1 can golden mushroom soup
1 cup dry sherry
1 cup green grapes

Place all ingredients in a buttered, covered ovenproof casserole. Bake for 1 hour, or until bubbly in 350° preheated oven.

Chicken & Chipped Beef

Preparation time: 5 minutes

Cooking time: 1 hour

Serves: 6

6 chicken breasts
1 cup mushroom soup
1 pint sour cream
1 package chipped beef in small pieces
1 can peas, drained
4 tablespoons butter

    Place breasts in 9" × 13" × 2" baking dish. Spread butter over chicken. Mix soup, sour cream, chipped beef and peas together. Pour over chicken. Bake uncovered in preheated 350° oven for 1 hour. Serve with hot rice or cooked egg noodles.

Chicken in Wine

Preparation time: 5 minutes

Cooking time: 2-1/2 hours

Serves: 6–8

6–8 chicken breasts
1 can mushroom soup, undiluted
1 can onion soup, undiluted
1 cup dry white wine

    Combine soups and wine in a large oven-proof covered casserole. Add chicken, stirring around to coat with sauce. Bake in preheated 300° oven for 2-1/2 hours, covered.

Chicken Livers Supreme

Preparation time: 15 minutes

Cooking time: 25 minutes

Serves: 3–4

2 tablespoons margarine
1 medium onion, chopped (3/4 cup)
1 jar (2-1/2 oz.) sliced mushrooms or, 4 large fresh mushrooms, sliced
3/4 pound chicken livers
1 carton (8 oz.) commercial sour cream
1 teaspoon paprika
1 teaspoon salt
1 teaspoon ground pepper

    Sauté onion and mushrooms in margarine until tender (5 minutes, approximately). Move onion-mushroom mixture to side of pan; add chicken livers to pan and brown them on all sides (approximately 5 minutes). Stir all together, cover, reduce heat and simmer for 10 minutes, stirring occasionally.

    Remove from heat. Add sour cream, paprika, salt and pepper and stir well. Return to stove. Cover and simmer for 5 additional minutes.

    Serve over hot cooked noodles.

Curried Chicken

Preparation time: 10 minutes

Cooking time: 40 minutes

Serves: 4

4 whole chicken breasts
all-purpose flour
melted shortening or cooking oil (approximately 3 tablespoons)
2 (10-3/4 oz. ea.) cans cream of chicken soup, undiluted
1 cup water
1/2 to 1-1/2 teaspoons curry powder (to taste)
1/2 cup toasted slivered almonds
hot cooked rice

    Dredge chicken with flour, and then brown chicken in hot oil in skillet. Combine soup, water, curry powder; pour over chicken. Cover skillet and simmer over low heat 40 minutes.
    Sprinkle with almonds (toast them first for 5 minutes in preheated 400° oven). Serve over hot rice.

Hot Chicken Sandwich

Preparation time: 10 minutes

Cooking time: 25–30 minutes, plus previously cooked chicken (30 minutes) and hard boiled eggs (15 minutes)

Serves: 8

16 slices Pepperidge Farm white bread
6 boned chicken breasts, cooked and cut into cubes* (approximately 2-1/2 cups)
3 hard-cooked eggs, chopped
1/3 cup chopped onions
1/4 to 1/2 cup chopped pitted black olives (3 oz. can)
1/2 cup freshly sliced mushrooms or 4 oz. can
3/4 cup mayonnaise
1 cup (8 oz.) commercially prepared sour cream
butter or margarine
1 (10-3/4 oz.) can cream of chicken soup

    Trim crusts from bread. Butter 8 slices of bread and place, butter side down, in 13" × 9" × 2" pyrex

Chicken, Fish and Cheese Dishes

baking dish. Mix together chicken, eggs, onions, olives, mushrooms, and mayonnaise. Spread evenly over the 8 slices of bread. Top with remaining 8 slices of bread. Cover all with combined soup and sour cream. Add a little milk to soup-sour cream topping if it is too thick. Bake in preheated 350° oven for approximately 25 minutes.

*See recipe for cooking chicken with Turkey Casserole recipe.

Manhattan-Style Chicken
(for Grill)

Preparation time: 10 minutes

Cooking time: 35–40 minutes (sauce)
     45–50 minutes (chicken)

Serves: 6

1 (6-1/2 oz.) *can minced clams*
1 (8 oz.) *bottle (1 cup) clam juice*
1 *cup catsup*
2 *tablespoons cooking oil*
1 *tablespoon Worcestershire sauce*
1 *tablespoon lemon juice*
1 *small onion (1/4 cup) finely chopped*
2 *tablespoons fresh snipped parsley, or dried parsley*
1 *3-1/2 pound chicken cut up or 6 large chicken breasts*
1 *clove garlic, minced*

Drain clams, reserving liquid. Set clams aside. In medium saucepan, combine clam liquid, clam juice, catsup, cooking oil, Worcestershire sauce, lemon juice, onion and garlic. Bring to a boil. Reduce heat, simmer, uncovered for 30–35 minutes. Stir in parsley and clams. Place chicken pieces, bone side down over medium-hot coals. Grill chicken for 25 minutes or until well-browned. Turn chicken. Grill 20–25 minutes more or until chicken is tender. Brush chicken often with sauce *during the last 10 minutes* of grilling. Pass remaining warm sauce with chicken.

Oriental Chicken

Preparation time: 5 minutes and marinate in refrigerator overnight

Cooking time: 1-1/2 hours

Serves: 4

4 large chicken breasts
1/2 cup honey
1/2 cup Dijon mustard
1 teaspoon curry powder
2 teaspoons soy sauce

Place chicken, skin side down, in flat baking dish. Mix ingredients and pour over chicken. Marinate overnight in refrigerator. When ready to bake, turn chicken, skin side up, and cover dish with foil. Bake in preheated 350° oven for 1-1/4 hours. Remove foil and bake 15 minutes more, basting chicken three or four times.

Oven-Fried Parmesan Chicken

Preparation time: 10 minutes

Cooking time: 1 hour

Serves: 4

1 cup round buttery cracker crumbs or 1 cup boxed cracker crumbs
1/2 cup grated Parmesan cheese
2 tablespoons freshly chopped parsley
1/2 teaspoon salt
1 (2-1/2–3 pound) boiler-fryer; cut up or 4 large chicken breasts
1/2 cup butter, melted

Combine first 4 ingredients; mix well. Dip chicken in butter, dredge in cracker crumb mixture. Place chicken in a lightly greased 13" × 9" × 2" baking dish. Bake uncovered, at 350° for 1 hour—skin side up. Do not turn over.

Chicken, Fish and Cheese Dishes

Turkey or Chicken Casserole

Preparation time: 15 minutes

Cooking time: 30 minutes

Serves: 4

1 can (16 oz.) *asparagus spears* (*drained*)
cooked turkey pieces or cooked boned chicken pieces (*approx. 2 cups*)
1 *package onion soup mix*
1 *pint sour cream*
1 *cup unsweetened whipped cream*
Parmesan cheese

Layer asparagus spears and turkey pieces in 2 quart pyrex casserole, then cover with half the onion soup and sour cream mixed together. Repeat layers, then cover with whipped cream and top with Parmesan cheese. Bake at 350° for around 30 minutes, or until slightly browned on top.

To cook chicken:

Preparation time: 5 minutes

Cooking time: 30–35 minutes (after it has started to simmer)

Cover 3 large or 4 medium chicken breasts* with water (about 3 cups) to which you have added 1/2 cup of sliced onions, 1 teaspoon salt, 1/2 of a bay leaf and 3 whole pepper corns. Simmer all for 30–35 minutes, or until chicken is tender. Remove bones and cut chicken into chunks.

*Save the "stock" after removing the chicken. Strain it and keep in refrigerator. (It freezes well.) For use in any dish that requires chicken stock or broth. You can also use the "boned" chicken pieces.

Baked Fish in Foil

Preparation time: 5 minutes

Chilling time: 1 hour

Cooking time: 35–45 minutes

Serves: 6

1 small garlic clove, peeled and minced
1 teaspoon salt
1/2 teaspoon oregano
1/2 teaspoon basil
1/2 teaspoon thyme leaves, crumbled
pepper to taste
1/3 cup melted butter
3 tablespoons chopped onion
3 tablespoons white wine or fresh lemon juice
1 cleaned whole fish, weighing 4 to 5 pounds, head and back fin removed
1 to 2 tablespoons fresh parsley or dill, minced

Mix together garlic, salt, oregano, basil, thyme and pepper. Stir in melted butter, onion and wine or lemon juice. Tear off a sheet of wide, heavy-duty aluminum foil cut twice the length of the fish plus 3 to 4 inches. Place sheet of foil in baking pan with half the piece extending over one end of pan.

Place fish on foil. Pour marinade over fish. Bring extending half of foil over fish and seal three sides with double folds. Refrigerate about one hour. Bake in preheated 350° oven 35 to 45 minutes, or until fish flakes easily with fork. Serve piping hot on heated platter. Garnish with parsley or dill.

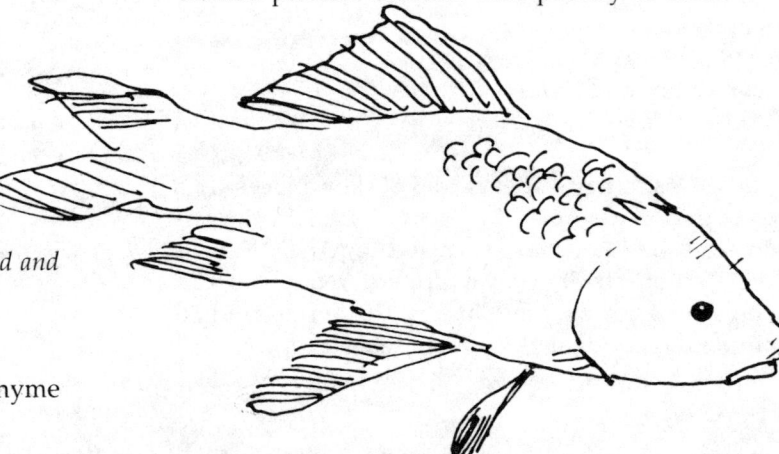

Chicken, Fish and Cheese Dishes

Fillet of Flounder or Sole
with mayonnaise topping

Preparation time: 5 minutes

Cooking time: 15–20 minutes

Serves: 4–6

1-1/2 to 2 pounds of fillet (sole or flounder)
mayonnaise—1/2 cup or more
salt & pepper to taste

Salt and pepper fish fillets. Coat well with mayonnaise (put on thickly as though you were frosting the top of a cake). Bake uncovered in a preheated 350° oven about 15 minutes or until fish flakes easily and top is lightly browned.

Fillet of Sole Gourmet

Preparation time: 10 minutes

Cooking time: 25 minutes

Serves: 6

2 pounds fillet of sole
4 tablespoons each of butter and olive oil
1/2 cup rosé wine
1-1/2 teaspoon ground basil
1/4 cup chopped parsley
1/2 cup onion, finely chopped
paprika

In an 8″ × 8″ baking dish, melt butter with olive oil in preheated 400° oven. Arrange fish in dish. Add wine. Sprinkle with rest of ingredients. Return to oven and bake uncovered for 25 minutes.

Fillet of Sole with Sour Cream

Preparation time: 15 minutes

Cooking time: 15 minutes

Serves: 6

2 pounds fillet of sole, sprinkle with salt & pepper
1/2 cup butter, softened
1/2 cup sour cream
1/4 cup chopped green onions
2 teaspoons dried parsley
1 clove garlic, mashed
3 tablespoons lemon juice
1/2 cup plain crackers, rolled into crumbs (*cracker crumbs can be purchased packaged*)

On a jelly roll/cookie sheet type of pan, arrange the fillets in one layer. Combine the next 6 ingredients and mix until blended. Spread this mixture over the fillets. Sprinkle the top evenly with the cracker crumbs. Bake in preheated 350° oven for about 15 minutes, or until fish flakes easily with a fork. Do not overcook.

Crabmeat/Artichoke Casserole

Preparation time: 20 minutes

Cooking time: 20 minutes (baking)

Serves: 4

1 14-1/2 oz. can artichoke hearts (*in water*), drained
1 lb. backfin fresh or canned crabmeat (*remove any shells*)
1/2 pound fresh mushrooms (1 cup)
6 tablespoons butter
2-1/2 tablespoons flour
1 cup light cream
1/2 teaspoon salt
1 teaspoon Worcestershire sauce
1/4 cup dry sherry
paprika, cayenne pepper, and black pepper, to taste
1/4 cup Parmesan cheese

    Place artichokes on bottom of 2-quart casserole dish (pyrex). Wipe 1 cup mushrooms with damp paper towel, slice thinly and sauté for 5 minutes in 2 tablespoons butter. Add to crabmeat. Melt 4 tablespoons butter in saucepan and add all remaining ingredients except Parmesan cheese, stirring well after each addition. Cook over medium flame, stirring constantly until sauce thickens (and just begins to boil). Pour over crabmeat. Sprinkle cheese on top. Bake in 375° preheated oven for 20 minutes.
    Serve with rice.

Crabmeat Au Gratin

Preparation time: 10 minutes

Cooking time: 20–30 minutes (baking)

Serves: 4

1/4 cup butter
1/4 cup flour
1 cup half & half
1 teaspoon salt
1/8 teaspoon pepper
1/4 cup sherry
1 pound backfin crabmeat (remove any shells)
3/4 cup Cheddar cheese, shredded
buttered breadcrumbs

Melt butter by low flame, stir in flour, then half & half, salt, pepper, and sherry until mixture thickens. Then add cheese and crabmeat. Pour mixture into buttered 1-1/2 quart pyrex baking dish. Top with bread crumbs and small bits of butter over top of all. Bake in preheated 375° oven for 20–30 minutes.

Crabmeat Mornay

Preparation time: 15 minutes

Cooking time: 10–15 minutes

Serves: 6

1 stick (4 oz.) butter or margarine
1 bunch green onions, chopped
1/2 cup chopped parsley
2 tablespoons flour
2 cups table cream
1/2 pound (2 cups) grated Swiss cheese
1 tablespoon dry sherry
1 pound lump crabmeat
red pepper to taste
salt to taste
patty shells or toast points

Melt butter or margarine in a heavy saucepot. Sauté onions and parsley for about 5 minutes. Blend in flour, slowly add cream; heat, stirring until thickened. Add cheese and stir until melted. Add sherry, red pepper and salt. Gently fold in crabmeat. Serve in patty shells or over toast points.

Tuna Casserole

Preparation time: 5 minutes

Cooking time: 30 minutes

Serves: 3

1 (13 oz.) can tuna, drained
1 (10 oz.) can condensed cream of mushroom soup
2 cups crushed potato chips
1 soup can milk

Preheat oven to 350°. Mix all ingredients together.* Put into pyrex casserole and bake for 30 minutes.

*Add more chips to casserole if it is too juicy, more milk if it is too dry.

Tuna Topside Down Pie

Preparation time: 10 minutes

Cooking time: 30 minutes

Serves: 6

6 thin lemon slices
large (13 oz.) can tuna, drained
1/2 cup soft bread crumbs
6 tablespoons milk
2 eggs, beaten
1/4 cup chopped parsley
1/2 cup golden Italian salad dressing
1 cup Bisquick

Arrange lemon slices on bottom of 8 or 9-inch pie plate. In a medium-sized bowl, blend everything except Bisquick and milk. In a small bowl, mix the Bisquick and milk with a fork. Put the tuna mixture over the lemon slices. Top all with the dough mixture. Bake in a preheated 400° oven for 30 minutes. Remove from oven. Invert onto serving plate.

Chicken, Fish and Cheese Dishes

Chilies Rellenos Casserole

Preparation time: 15 minutes and refrigerate overnight

Cooking time: 50–55 minutes

Serves: 4–6

6 slices bread
butter or margarine, softened
2 cups (1/2 lb.) shredded Cheddar cheese
2 cups shredded Monterey Jack cheese (1/2 lb.)
1/4 teaspoon garlic powder
1/4 teaspoon dry mustard
1 4 oz. can green chilies, chopped
6 eggs
2 cups milk
2 teaspoons salt
1/2 teaspoon pepper
2 teaspoons paprika
1 teaspoon whole oregano

Trim crusts from bread. Spread one side of each slice with butter; place buttered side down in 13" × 9" × 2" baking dish. Top with Cheddar and Monterey Jack cheese; sprinkle with chilies.

Beat eggs until frothy; add remaining ingredients, mix well. Pour egg mixture over bread and cheese mixture in baking dish. Cover and chill overnight, or at least 4 hours.

Uncover and bake in 325° preheated oven for 50–55 minutes or until lightly browned. Let stand 10 minutes before serving.

Feather-Light Cheese Puff

Preparation time: 15 minutes

Cooking time: 55–60 minutes

Serves: 4 to 6

35 crispy butter crackers (1 stack pack), coarsely broken
8 oz. grated sharp Cheddar cheese (about 2 cups)
2 tablespoons butter or margarine
1/4 pound mushrooms, sliced
4 eggs, lightly beaten
2-1/2 cups milk
1 small onion, minced (1/4 cup)
2 tablespoons parsley
1/4 teaspoon poultry seasoning

    Sprinkle cracker crumbs evenly in generously greased 1-1/2 or 2 quart soufflé dish. Cover with grated cheese; set aside.
    In medium skillet, melt butter or margarine; add mushrooms and cook until limp, about four minutes. Spoon mushrooms on top of cheese. In medium bowl, beat eggs with milk, onion, parsley and poultry seasoning. Pour evenly over mixture in soufflé dish. Bake at 350° 55 to 60 minutes, until puffed and lightly browned. Serve at once.

Impossible Quiche

Preparation time: 15 minutes

Cooking time: 10 minutes (bacon)
                    50–55 minutes (quiche)

Serves: 4–5

12 slices bacon (quarter each slice), crisply fried
1 cup shredded Swiss cheese (about 4 oz.)
1/2 cup Bisquick
2 cups milk
1/3 cup finely chopped onion
4 large eggs
1/4 teaspoon salt
1/4 teaspoon freshly ground pepper

Chicken, Fish and Cheese Dishes

Lightly grease a 9 or 10-inch pie plate or quiche dish. Crumble bacon. Sprinkle it and the cheese and onion evenly over the bottom of plate. Place remaining ingredients in blender. Cover and blend at high speed for one minute. Pour over bacon, cheese and onion mixture. Bake in preheated 350° oven for about 50 to 55 minutes or until golden brown and a knife inserted in center comes out clean. Let stand 5 minutes before serving. Refrigerate any leftover quiche.

Skillet Cheese Toast

Preparation time: 5 minutes

Cooking time: 8 minutes (5 minutes on stove, 3 minutes in broiler)

Serves: 4

1 8 oz. package Muenster cheese, shredded
1 tablespoon prepared Dijon mustard
1 teaspoon Worcestershire sauce
1 egg
4 tablespoons butter or margarine
8 1-inch thick diagonal slices of Italian bread
1/2 pint cherry tomatoes

Preheat broiler. In small bowl, mix cheese, mustard, Worcestershire sauce and egg.

In a 12-inch skillet with broiler-safe handle (or cover skillet handle with heavy-duty foil) over medium-low heat, cook bread in hot butter or margarine; cook until golden brown on one side. Remove skillet from heat. Turn bread, top each slice with some cheese mixture.

Place skillet in broiler, broil until cheese mixture is hot and bubbly, about 3 minutes. Garnish with cherry tomatoes.

Spinach Quiche

Preparation time: 15 minutes

Cooking time: 5 minutes (pie shell)
  about 6 minutes (spinach)
  30–35 minutes (quiche)

Serves: 4–5

partially baked (5 minutes at 400°) 9-inch pie shell
2 tablespoons butter
1 green onion (scallion), minced
1 cup chopped cooked spinach
3/4 teaspoon salt
nutmet & freshly ground pepper to taste
4 large eggs
2 cups cream or *half and half* or *milk*
1/3 cup grated Swiss cheese

Sauté the green onion in the butter for a few minutes, then add the finely chopped, cooked, well-drained spinach. Cook over moderate heat until any excess water has evaporated (another minute or two). Stir in salt, pepper and nutmeg. Set aside to cool.

Beat together the eggs and cream or milk. Stir in the spinach mixture. Taste for seasoning.

Pour into partially baked pie shell. Sprinkle with grated Swiss cheese.

Bake in preheated 375° oven for 30–35 minutes or until the quiche puffs up and a knife inserted into the center comes out clean.

Super Cream Sauce
(for meat, poultry or eggs)

Preparation time: 10 minutes

Cooking time: 10 minutes

Serves: 3–4

1/4 cup chopped onions
1 tablespoon margarine
1/4 cup milk
1 (8 oz.) package cream cheese, cubed
2-1/2 oz. jar mushrooms, drained
1/4 cup grated Parmesan cheese
2 tablespoons chopped parsley
*Meat, Poultry or Eggs

   Sauté onion in margarine. Add milk and cream cheese; stir over low heat until cream cheese melts. Stir in mushrooms, Parmesan cheese and parsley.

*Any of the following can be added:
6 hard boiled eggs cut into eighths, or 1 pound round steak, cut in strips and browned in margarine or oil, or leftover cooked chicken or turkey, cubed, or 1 3 oz. package smoked sliced beef. Serve any of these in sauce over toasted English muffins, toast points, or patty shells.

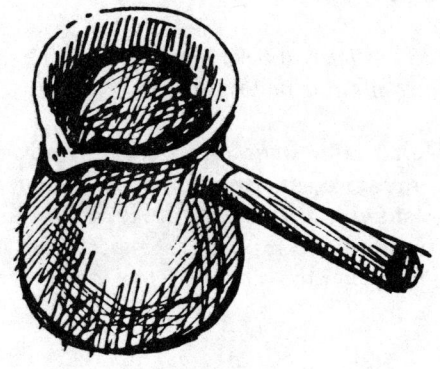

Welsh Rarebit

Preparation time: 10 minutes (includes cooking)

Cooking time: approximately 7 minutes

Serves: 4

1 tablespoon butter or margarine
1-1/2 pounds sharp aged cheese (Cheddar), diced
1 teaspoon fine hot mustard
8 oz. dark beer
cayenne pepper to taste (not too much!)
English muffins or toast points

 Melt butter over low heat and add the cheese and mustard, stirring constantly. As it melts, add beer slowly, stirring the mixture so the beer is incorporated and mixture is smooth. Stir in cayenne.
 Serve over toast or crisp toasted English muffins.

Beef, Lamb, Pork and Veal

Beef Stroganoff

Preparation time: 20 minutes

Cooking time: 30 minutes

Serves: 4–6

2 pounds round steak, cubed
1 clove garlic, chopped—1/2 cup onion, chopped
2 tablespoons butter
1/2 cup beef broth
2 tablespoons flour
1/4 cup red wine
1 teaspoon Dijon mustard
1 cup sour cream (commercial)
1 pound mushrooms, cut in half
Salt & ground pepper (1/2 teaspoon each or to taste)
Cooked hot noodles

Sauté onions and garlic in butter until yellow (5 minutes). Add cubes of beef and brown. Add beef broth (either canned broth or use beef bouillion cube dissolved in 1/2 cup hot water), flour, wine, mustard, and salt and pepper. Stir in sour cream. Simmer for 25 minutes. Add mushrooms and cook for about 3 minutes longer. Serve over hot noodles. Sprinkle with paprika.

Beefy Beans

Preparation time: 15 minutes

Cooking time: 30 minutes

Serves: 4–6

1 pound ground beef
2 cups chopped celery
1/2 cup chopped onion
1 (16 oz.) can whole tomatoes
2 (16 oz. each) cans pork and beans
1/2 cup catsup
1/3 cup firmly packed brown sugar
1/4 cup Worcestershire sauce
1 tablespoon lemon juice
1/4 teaspoon salt
1/4 teaspoon pepper

Combine ground beef, celery, and onion in a large skillet; cook until meat is browned and vegetables are tender. Drain mixture well. Stir in remaining ingredients; cover and simmer 30 minutes.

Brisket of Beef

Preparation time: 5 minutes

Cooking time: 2 hours, 45 minutes to 3 hours

Serves: 8–10

1 (6–8 pound) whole brisket
1 package Lipton onion soup mix
1/2 teaspoon each salt & pepper
1/2 teaspoon garlic powder
1/2 teaspoon onion powder

Wash brisket under running cold water. Pat dry with paper towel. Place in large roasting pan. Sprinkle with salt, pepper, onion and garlic powders. Sprinkle onion soup mix on top of brisket and all around pan. Add sufficient water to cover about 1/3 of brisket. Put in preheated 325° oven for 45 minutes, uncovered. Baste and cover. Roast for about 2 hours longer or until tender. Remove from oven and cool. Slice thinly and lay back in gravy.

Can be made up to 3 days in advance.

Chili & Corn Chips

Preparation time: 10 minutes

Cooking time: 15–20 minutes

Serves: 5

1 medium bag corn chips
1 large (40 oz.) can chili with beans
1 8 oz. can tomato sauce
1 small onion, chopped
1 cup sharp Cheddar cheese

Preheat oven to 375°.
Cover bottom of 7" × 11" × 1-1/2" casserole dish with 1/2 package of corn chips. Spread chili over chips. Pour tomato sauce and chopped onion on top. Sprinkle with corn chips. Top with grated cheese. Bake at 375° 15 to 20 minutes.
Top with sour cream if desired.

Cube Steak Italiano

Preparation time: 15 minutes

Cooking time: 15 minutes

Serves: 4

1 pound cube steak
1 large onion
1 green pepper
2 tablespoons salad oil
1 cup bottled (or canned) spaghetti sauce
salt and pepper to taste
cooked pasta or rice

Slice steak, onion and green pepper into strips. Sauté all in 2 tablespoons salad oil about 5 minutes, or until the meat is brown. Stir in 1 cup bottled spaghetti sauce, salt and pepper; cover, simmer for 10 minutes. Serve over cooked noodles or rice.

Cowboy Stew

Preparation time: 20–25 minutes

Cooking time: 45 minutes

Serves: 6–8

6 slices bacon
1 cup sliced onion (1 large onion)
1/2 cup chopped green pepper
1 clove of garlic, crushed
1-1/2 pounds ground round or chuck
1 can (1 pound, 3 oz.) tomatoes
1 teaspoon salt
1/2 teaspoon freshly ground pepper
1 tablespoon chili powder
1 can (12 oz.) whole kernel corn, drained
1 can (about 1 lb.) red kidney beans, drained
2 cups cubed pared potatoes

Cook bacon until crisp; drain on paper towels; crumble; reserve. Sauté onion, green pepper and crushed garlic in bacon drippings until tender. Add ground beef; cook until well-browned, breaking up with a fork as it cooks. Add tomatoes, salt, pepper, chili powder; cover; simmer 30 minutes. Add drained corn, drained kidney beans, and cubed potatoes; simmer 15 minutes (or until potatoes are tender).

Sprinkle with bacon.

Ground Beef Skillet Dinner

Preparation time: 15 minutes

Cooking time: 25 minutes

Serves: 4

1 pound ground beef
1 cup chopped onion
1 cup chopped green pepper
3 cups tomato juice
1 (5 oz.) package egg noodles
1–1-1/2 teaspoon salt
1 teaspoon celery salt
2 teaspoons Worcestershire sauce
1/2 teaspoon freshly ground pepper
1 cup commercial sour cream

   Cook ground beef, onion, and green pepper over medium heat in a skillet until meat is browned, stirring to crumble meat. Drain well.

Stir in remaining ingredients, except sour cream; cover and simmer 20 to 25 minutes. Stir in sour cream and cook until heated (do not boil).

Hamburger with Cream-Cognac Sauce

Preparation time: 5 minutes

Cooking time: approximately 20 minutes

Serves: 2

1/2 pound hamburger
Dijon mustard
2 teaspoons butter
4 tablespoons table cream
2 tablespoons cognac
pepper to taste

Form two patties from hamburger. Paint each burger on both sides with Dijon mustard (French mustard mixed with wine and vinegar, available in grocery stores).

Melt butter over medium heat in skillet. Sauté patties 7 minutes on one side, then turn and sauté 7 minutes on the other for a rare burger.

Remove burgers to a warm plate and drain grease from skillet, reserving the brown bits that have accumulated in the pan.

Return pan to heat and add cream and cognac. Stir constantly until sauce thickens and turns a golden yellow. Serve over patties.

Heavenly Brisket

Preparation time: 5 minutes

Cooking time: 3 to 3-1/2 hours

Serves: 8 to 10

7 to 8 pounds first cut brisket of beef
4 bay leaves
2 teaspoons thyme leaves
4 tablespoons catsup
4 tablespoons prepared mustard

Put beef brisket in shallow roasting pan. Cover the top of roast with mustard and catsup in a swirling motion. Sprinkle thyme on brisket; put bay leaves around the roast. Cover pan with aluminum foil. Put brisket in preheated 350° oven for 1/2 hour. Lower oven temperature to 325° and bake for 2-1/2 to 3 hours more or until fork test shows meat to be tender. Slice thin and serve.

Marinated Flank Steak
(for outdoor grill)*

Preparation time: 5 minutes
Refrigeration time: overnight
Cooking time: 15–20 minutes on grill
Serves: 6–8

1/2 cup soy sauce (*Kikamon brand, if available*)
1/2 cup honey
1/2 cup water
1 cup dry *vermouth*
6 scallions, diced
3 cloves garlic, minced or crushed
2 flank steaks (*large to serve 6–8 people, about 3 lbs.*)

Combine first 6 ingredients in a bowl. Score the steak on both sides and place in a plastic food storage bag. Poor marinade into bag all over steak. Push out most air and secure bag tightly with a bag tie. Marinate in refrigerator for overnight, *turning bag occasionally*. Broil steaks on preheated grill 7–10 minutes on each side, basting with marinade often. Leftover marinade may be heated and used to cook sliced mushrooms or to serve with meat, if desired.

*Can also be cooked in oven broiler—about 5–7 minutes on each side.

Meat Loaf

Preparation time: 10 minutes
Cooking time: 1 hour
Serves: 4–6

2 pounds ground beef
    or
2 pounds ground beef/veal/pork combo
2 slices of bread (*cubed*)
1 large egg, slightly beaten
1 tablespoon Worcestershire sauce
1/2 cup catsup

Beef, Lamb, Pork and Veal

1 teaspoon salt
3 tablespoons parsley
1/2 cup chopped onion
1/2 teaspoon ground pepper

Sauce:

1 cup catsup
2 tablespoons brown sugar
2 dashes Tabasco sauce

Combine all ingredients, mix thoroughly. Place in a 3-quart, greased, pyrex baking dish and bake uncovered in preheated 350° oven for 45 minutes. Put sauce on top of meat and return to oven for another 15 minutes.

Open-Face Reuben Sandwich

Preparation time: 5 minutes

Cooking time: 5–10 minutes

Serves: 1

1 slice Jewish rye bread
1/4 pound (or more) Kosher deli corned beef
2–3 tablespoons canned sauerkraut
1 slice Swiss cheese

Sauce:

4 tablespoons mayonnaise mixed with 1 tablespoon chili sauce or catsup

Preheat broiler of oven. When ready to serve sandwich, layer as follows: bread, then corned beef, then sauerkraut, then cheese. Top all with mayonnaise sauce. Broil for 5 to 10 minutes, or until slightly brown and bubbly.

Perfect Roast Beef

Preparation time: 1 minute

Cooking time: 4 hours and 20 minutes

Serves: depends on size of roast—allow 1/2 pound per person

1 roast—*sirloin tip or rolled cross rib or rolled chuck (at least 3 pounds of meat), salt & pepper*

Roast should be at room temperature, so take it out of refrigerator first thing in the morning. Place roast on a rack in a shallow baking pan.

4 hours and 20 minutes before you wish to serve roast, put it in a preheated 375° oven for 1 hour. Then *turn off* the oven but *do not* open the oven door; if you do, you'll let the heat out and ruin the whole process. Trust me, it works. Do not open the oven!

Allow 3 hours in (turned off) oven to complete the cooking. You can even let it go a bit longer if need be. About 20 minutes before you want dinner on the table, turn the oven back on to 300° to warm up roast. *Now* oven can be opened and serve roast.

Pizza Beef Pie

Preparation time: 10 minutes

Cooking time: 20 to 22 minutes

Serves: 4–6

1-1/2 pounds ground beef (*chuck*)
1/2 teaspoon garlic salt
1 egg, slightly beaten
8 oz. can tomato sauce
1/2 cup chopped onions (*more, if desired*)
1/4 teaspoon oregano
Parmesan cheese

   Mix together 2 tablespoons of the tomato sauce and the ground beef, egg, onion, and garlic salt. Press this mixture into a 9-inch pie plate (on bottom and sides of plate). Bake in preheated 450° oven for 10 to 12 minutes. Remove from oven and sprinkle 1/4 teaspoon oregano and the rest of the tomato sauce. Top all with lots of Parmesan cheese and return to oven for 10 minutes more.

Spicy Meat Loaf

Preparation time: 10 minutes

Cooking time: 1-1/2 hours

Serves: 6–8

2 pounds ground chuck
1 (10-1/2 oz.) can vegetable soup, undiluted
1/2 cup commercial sour cream
1/4 cup regular oats, uncooked
1/4 cup chopped green pepper
1/4 cup chopped onion
1 (1.5 ounce) package spaghetti sauce mix
1 tablespoon minced parsley
1 teaspoon prepared mustard
1/2 cup catsup

   Combine all ingredients except catsup. Spoon mixture into a well-greased 9" × 5" × 3" casserole. Spoon catsup over meat. Bake in preheated 350° oven for 1-1/2 hours. Let stand 10 minutes before removing from pan.

Sweet & Sour Beef

Preparation time: 10 minutes

Cooking time: 1 hour 5 minutes

Serves: 5

1/2 cup chopped onions
1/3 cup brown sugar
1/3 cup vinegar
1 can (16 oz.) tomato sauce
1/8 teaspoon garlic powder
salt and ground pepper to taste (1/2 teaspoon each or more)
2 green peppers
2 pounds beef cubes
1/4 cup cooking oil

Brown beef cubes in oil. Add all ingredients except green pepper. Cook in covered skillet or electric fry pan on "simmer" for 1 hour or until meat is tender. Add a little water during cooking if necessary.

When meat is tender, add green pepper that has been cut in strips (remove core of pepper and discard). Cook several minutes more.
Serve over hot rice or cooked egg noodles.

Teriyaki Flank Steak

Preparation time: 5 minutes

Cooking time: marinate 6 hours or overnight broil 10–20 minutes (5–10 minutes each side)

Serves: 4

2 tablespoons soy sauce (Kikoman)
2 tablespoons honey
2 tablespoons dry sherry
1 tablespoon red wine vinegar
1/2 teaspoon ginger
dash of garlic powder
1 flank steak (about 2 pounds)
1 can (8-1/4 oz.) pineapple slices

Stir together soy sauce, honey, sherry, vinegar, ginger and garlic powder. Pour mixture over flank steak in shallow baking dish. Allow to marinate 6 hours or overnight in refrigerator. Remove steak from marinade, reserving marinade. Broil steak over hot coals or in broiler of oven 5 minutes on each side for rare, or longer, to desired doneness. Two minutes before end of broiling, dip pineapple slices in marinade and broil with steak. Brush steak with reserved marinade during cooking.

Lamb Steaks or Chops

Preparation time: 10 minutes

Cooking time: 10 minutes (sauce)
10–14 minutes (lamb)

Serves: 4

1 tablespoon butter
1-1/2 teaspoon sugar
1-1/2 to 2 teaspoons curry powder
1/4 cup chicken broth or bouillon
4 lamb sirloin chops, steaks or shoulder chops about 3/4 to 1 inch thick
salt & pepper

In a small saucepan, melt butter. Blend in sugar and curry powder. Stir in chicken broth or bouillon. Cook over low heat, stirring occasionally, for 3 to 4 minutes. Arrange lamb sirloin chops, steaks or shoulder chops on grill rack. Brush lamb with half of the curry mixture. Broil or grill 3 to 4 inches from source of heat 5 to 7 minutes. Turn and sprinkle with salt and pepper to taste. Brush with remaining curry mixture. Broil 5 to 7 minutes, or until desired degree of doneness.

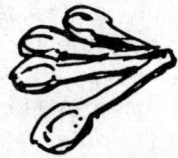

Curried Ham and Peaches

Preparation time: 5 minutes

Cooking time: 15 minutes

Serves: 2 large or 4 small servings

1 (16 oz.) *can peach halves*
1 *tablespoon margarine*
2 or 4 *slices cooked ham* (*about a total of 1 pound*)
1-1/2–2 *teaspoons curry powder*
2 *tablespoons brown sugar*
another tablespoon of margarine

    Drain peach halves, reserving syrup (set aside.)
    Melt 1 tablespoon margarine in a large skillet. Brown ham in margarine; remove and set aside. Add peach syrup and curry powder to pan drippings. Place peach halves, cut side down, in syrup mixture; cook over medium heat for 2 minutes. Turn peaches; fill cavities with brown sugar and dot with remaining margarine. Return ham to skillet, cover and cook 3 minutes.

Glazed Orange Pork Chops

Preparation time: 10 minutes

Cooking time: 40 minutes

Serves: 4

4 *pork chops* (*about 1 pound*)
4 *slices of orange*
cinnamon
nutmeg
1 *can* (10-1/2 oz.) *condensed beef broth*
1 *tablespoon brown sugar*
2 *tablespoons orange juice*
1 *tablespoon cornstarch*

    Brown chops on both sides. Place an orange slice on each chop; sprinkle lightly with cinnamon and nutmeg. Add beef broth and brown sugar. Cover skillet and cook over low heat 35 minutes. Mix orange juice and cornstarch until smooth; gradually blend into broth. Cook stirring constantly until slightly thickened. Simmer a few minutes or until chops are tender.

Maple Sauce and Chops
(for grill)

Preparation time: 10 minutes

Cooking time: 35 minutes (sauce)
30–35 minutes (chops)

Serves: 4

1 cup catsup
1 cup maple-flavored syrup
3/4 cup dry white wine
1/4 cup water
1 teaspoon instant beef bouillon granules
1 bay leaf
2 garlic cloves, minced
1/4 teaspoon ground ginger
1 teaspoon dried thyme, crushed
1/2 teaspoon dried basil, crushed
1/2 teaspoon chili powder
1/2 teaspoon dry mustard
1/2 teaspoon salt
1/4 teaspoon freshly ground pepper
1/8 teaspoon ground cloves
4 pork loin chops, cut 1-1/2 inches thick

In saucepan combine all ingredients except chops. Bring to boiling. Reduce heat; simmer, uncovered, 30 minutes, stirring occasionally. Grill chops over medium coals for 20 minutes. Turn chops; grill 10 to 15 minutes more, brushing sauce over chops occasionally. To keep sauce warm, place in saucepan, on grill.

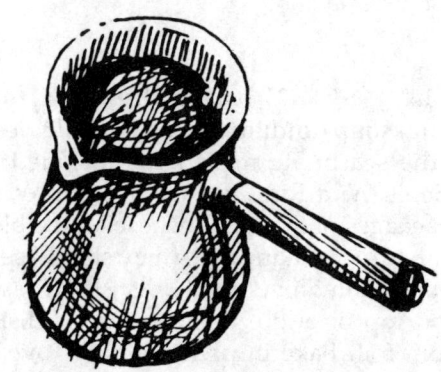

One Dish Meal—Pork Chops

Preparation time: 5 minutes

Cooking time: 1-1/4 hours

Serves: 5 (2 chops each)

10 pork chops—1/2 to 3/4 inch thick
1 package Uncle Ben's Wild Rice
1 can mushroom soup
2 packages Birds Eye Frozen Japanese Vegetables (or Chinese Vegetables)
1/2 cup water

In a 13" × 9" × 2" baking dish, mix together mushroom soup (undiluted) and the wild rice. Add to this the seasoning mix that is included in the Uncle Ben's Wild Rice box and 1/2 cup of water. Open packages of Frozen Japanese Vegetables and add to mixture in baking dish (they should separate and be distributed over entire dish). Put raw pork chops on top of entire mixture. Cover dish with aluminum foil. Bake in preheated 350° oven for 1 hour. Uncover and bake 15 minutes more or until chops are brown, adding a little more water if vegetable mixture is too dry.

Orange Glaze Pork Roast

Preparation time: 5 minutes

Cooking time: approximately 2 hours

Serves: 6–8

4 to 5 pound pork roast (have butcher "crack" the bone)
1 (8 oz.) can frozen orange juice, defrosted
dried oregano
garlic salt
basil leaves
1 bay leaf, crumbled
salt
freshly ground pepper

Wrap roast loosely with aluminum foil.
Pour defrosted concentrated orange juice over roast. Sprinkle roast with rest of ingredients. Seal foil around roast. Bake in preheated 375° oven for approximately 2 hours or until done.

Pork Chop, Apple & Cabbage Skillet

Preparation time: 15 minutes

Cooking time: 30 minutes

Serves: 4

4 medium pork chops, excess fat trimmed
2 tart, unpeeled, green or red apples, cored and thinly sliced
1 pound red or green cabbage thinly sliced
1 large onion, thinly sliced
4 to 6 teaspoons ground cumin
1/4 cup fresh lemon juice
freshly ground pepper to taste

    Brown chops on both sides in heavy skillet in a little of the trimmed fat over medium high heat. When chops are browned, remove from skillet. Drain off excess fat. Add apples, cabbage, onion, cumin, lemon juice and pepper. Return chops to skillet and cook covered, until chops are tender and vegetables are soft, about 30 minutes. Stir occasionally.

Pork Chops Cacciatore

Preparation time: 15 minutes

Cooking time: 1-1/4–1-1/2 hours

Serves: 6

6 pork chops—3/4 inch thick
1/2 teaspoon salt
6 thin large onion slices
1 envelope spaghetti sauce mix
2 cups tomatoes (16 oz. can)
1 tablespoon brown sugar
6 green pepper rings (2 medium peppers)

    Trim fat from chops. Heat fat in a large skillet; when you have about 1 tablespoon melted fat, remove trimmings. Brown chops on both sides. Season with salt and pepper. Place in 9" × 13" × 2" baking dish. Top each chop with onion slice. Combine sauce mix, tomatoes and brown sugar; pour over chops. Cover with foil and bake in preheated 350° oven for 1 hour. Remove foil and top chops with green pepper. Bake (uncovered dish) for another 15 minutes. Serve with hot cooked rice.

Pork Chops Hungarian

Preparation time: 10 minutes

Cooking time: 1 hour

Serves: 2

2 (3/4 inch thick each) loin pork chops
salad oil
1 small onion, thinly sliced (1/4 cup)
1/4 teaspoon caraway seeds
1/4 teaspoon salt
1/4 teaspoon paprika
1/8 teaspoon dillweed
dash of garlic powder
1/3 cup water (add more during cooking, if necessary)
1/3 cup commercial sour cream

Brown pork chops in a small amount of hot oil, drain. Add onion, caraway seeds, salt, paprika, dillweed, garlic powder and water. Cover and simmer over low heat about one hour or until chops are tender. Remove chops from pan. Add sour cream to meat drippings; blend well. Heat thoroughly but do not boil; spoon over chops.

Sweet and Sour Pork

Preparation time: 10 minutes

Cooking time: 15 minutes

Serves: 4

1 pound boneless pork, cut in strips
1 tablespoon cooking oil
1 tablespoon cornstarch
1 8 oz. can pineapple chunks in juice
1/4 cup vinegar
1/4 cup light brown sugar
1 tablespoon soy sauce
1/2 cup tomato sauce
1 green pepper, cut in strips

Brown pork in oil in a large skillet. Remove meat and set aside. Mix cornstarch with juice from pineapple. Add to skillet. Add vinegar, brown sugar and soy sauce. Stir over low heat until sauce thickens. Add pineapple chunks and pork. Bring to boil; simmer 5 minutes. Add tomato sauce and green pepper and cook a few minutes to heat through.

Serve over hot rice.

Veal and Peppers Rosemary

Preparation time: 5 minutes

Cooking time: 1 hour

Serves: 4

1 can (16 oz.) stewed tomatoes
1 teaspoon tomato paste
1 medium sized onion, sliced (3/4 cup)
1 green pepper, seeded and cubed
1 pound veal, cubed
1/2 teaspoon rosemary
1/4 teaspoon salt
1/2 teaspoon freshly ground pepper
2 cups cooked rice

Preheat oven to 350°. Empty stewed tomatoes into a casserole with a tight lid. Add tomato paste, onion, green pepper, veal, rosemary, salt and pepper. Mix well. Cover tightly and bake one hour, or until veal is tender. Serve over hot cooked rice.

Veal with White Wine

Preparation time: 10 minutes

Cooking time: 15 minutes

Serves: 4

2 pounds thinly sliced veal cutlets
1 package onion sauce (gravy) mix
1/2 cup water
1/4 pound butter
1/2 cup dry white wine
1/2 teaspoon salt
1 teaspoon lemon juice
1 tablespoon chopped parsley
1/4 pound mushrooms, sliced

Cut veal into 2-inch strips. Place veal and onion sauce mix in a paper bag and shake to mix, coating veal thoroughly. Sauté veal in butter until brown on both sides. Add mushrooms, water, wine and salt. Simmer 10 minutes. Stir in lemon juice and parsley.

Desserts

Baking Tips

Stiff Egg Whites & Meringues:

Egg whites should be room temperature before beating.

Meringue should always touch edge of pie crust to prevent shrinkage.

Put pie on middle shelf of oven so meringue will brown evenly.

When *almost* as brown as you want it, turn off oven and open door *slightly* so it will cool slowly, preventing meringue from cracking.

Always test to see that sugar is *completely* dissolved before cooking. Do this by putting some of it between two fingertips and rub them together, or put a bit on top of your tongue and rub it on the roof of your mouth and feel any undissolved sugar. If you feel any grains of sugar, beat some more.

Use a *large* rubber spatula when folding whites into a batter.

Do not overbeat egg whites. Stiff whites should have a glossy sheen. If they look powdery and granular, they have been overbeaten and will not rise or last.

Whipped Cream:

Use regular, pasteurized (*not* ultrapasteurized) heavy cream.

Cream should stand 3 or 4 days in refrigerator before you whip it. If it is within 3 days of its expiration date (*always* check expiration date of dairy products), letting it stand is not necessary.

Mixing bowl, beater and cream should be very cold. Chill bowl in refrigerator or freezer; stainless steel will chill the fastest.

Always add confectioner's sugar to whipped cream for topping desserts when recipe calls for sugar. Never use granulated sugar, as it will melt.

Desserts

To have whipped cream that will stay firm without weeping, beat it slowly at first, then gradually increase speed. It should take about 12 minutes to whip one pint of cream.

Adding Dry & Wet Ingredients:

When adding alternately to a batter, it is best to begin and end with dry ingredients. The mixture will grab better in the bowl and be more thoroughly blended.

To keep opened box of brown sugar soft:

Refrigerate with a slice of apple inside package. If the sugar should become hard, place a dampened paper towel in the package. Sugar will soften within a short time.

Cakes

Single cake—place rack in center of oven and put pan in center of rack.

Two layers—place rack in center of oven and put pans in opposite corners (one in rear left corner; one in front right corner).

Loaf or Tube pan—place rack in lower third of oven. Place pan in center of rack.

Store frosted cakes in a covered cake keeper or in refrigerator.

Unfrosted cakes may be wrapped in Saran Wrap or aluminum foil and stored at room temperature.

Caramel Orange Ring

Preparation time: 10 minutes

Cooking time: 30–40 minutes

Serves: 6–8

1 tablespoon sweet butter, softened
1/2 cup orange marmalade
2 tablespoons chopped nuts
1/2 to 3/4 cup firmly packed brown sugar (*depending on whether you like very "gooey" sticky buns*)
1/2 teaspoon cinnamon
2 (10 oz. each) cans refrigerated Buttermilk Flaky Biscuits (*Pillsbury*)
1/2 cup sweet butter, melted

Grease a 12-cup Bundt pan with 1 tablespoon butter. (Do not use a removable-bottom tube pan. A 3-quart ring mold may be substituted for a 12-cup Bundt pan.) Place, one teaspoon at a time, orange marmalade in pan. (There are about 12 teaspoonfuls to be distributed.) Sprinkle with nuts. In a small bowl, combine brown sugar and cinnamon. Mix well; set aside. Separate biscuits. Dip biscuits in melted butter, then in sugar mixture. Stand biscuits on edge of pan, spacing evenly. Sprinkle with remaining sugar mixture and drizzle with remaining butter. Bake in preheated 350° oven, near center of the oven, for 30 to 40 minutes, or until brown. Cool upright in pan for 5 minutes; invert onto serving plate.

Desserts

Electric Skillet Coffee Cake

Preparation time: 15 minutes

Cooking time: 30 minutes

Serves: 8 to 10

Cake

1 cup granulated sugar
2 eggs, beaten
1 (8 oz.) carton commercial sour cream
1-1/2 cup all-purpose flour
2 teaspoons baking powder
1/2 teaspoon soda
1 teaspoon salt

Topping

1/2 cup firmly packed brown sugar
2 tablespoons all-purpose flour
2 teaspoons ground cinnamon
1 teaspoon vanilla extract
2 tablespoons melted butter
1/2 cup chopped walnuts or pecans
4 tablespoons butter to dot cake & topping after baking

Cake
Grease an electric skillet; preheat to 280°. Combine sugar, eggs and sour cream; combine dry ingredients and add to sugar mixture, mixing well. Pour into electric skillet; cover and cook with vent closed for 30 minutes or until top of cake is almost dry. Sprinkle with topping. Dot with 4 tablespoons butter; cover and turn off heat. Let stand for 10 minutes before cutting.

Topping
Combine all the ingredients, except butter, to be used in dotting the cake.

Bourbon Chocolate Chip Pecan Pie

Preparation time: 10 minutes

Cooking time: 40–45 minutes

Serves: 6–8

1/4 cup butter (4 tablespoons), softened
1 cup sugar (granulated)
3 large eggs
3/4 cup light corn syrup
1 teaspoon vanilla
1/2 teaspoon salt
1/2 cup chocolate chips
1/2 cup pecans (pecan halves)
2 tablespoons bourbon (or rum)
10 inch pie shell—unbaked

   Beat softened butter and sugar. Add eggs, corn syrup, vanilla and salt. Stir in chocolate chips and bourbon. Pour into shell. Arrange pecans on top. Bake in preheated 375° oven for 40–45 minutes.
   Optional—top with whipped cream.

Brickle Ice Cream Pie and Sauce

Preparation time: 10 minutes

Chilling & Freezing time: minimum—2 hours

Serves: 8

Pie

prepared 9 inch graham cracker pie shell
1/2 gallon vanilla ice cream, softened to spoon easily, but not melted
1/2 of 7.8 oz. bag "Heath's Bits 'O Brickle"

Sauce

1-1/2 cups granulated sugar
1 cup evaporated milk
1/4 cup butter
1/4 cup light corn syrup
dash of salt
remaining 1/2 bag of Bits 'O Brickle

Pie

Spoon half of softened ice cream into prepared pie shell. Sprinkle 1/2 bag Bits 'O Brickle on top. Heap with remaining ice cream. Freeze.

Sauce

Combine sugar, milk, butter, syrup and salt. Bring to a boil over low heat; boil 1 minute. Remove from heat and stir in remaining 1/2 bag of Bits 'O Brickle. Cool, stirring occasionally. Chill.

To Serve

Stir sauce well, then spoon over individual pie wedges.

Remaining sauce may be refrigerated in a tightly covered container for use as a topping.

Chocolate Mousse Pie

Preparation time: 10 minutes

Chilling time: minimum—2 hours

Serves: 6

1 8 oz. package cream cheese
1 cup heavy cream
2 packages (3-1/2 oz. each) chocolate instant pudding
2 cups milk
1/2 cup Kahlúa
1/2 cup granulated sugar
1 teaspoon vanilla
1 9 inch graham cracker crust

Beat all ingredients on high speed of electric beater until mixture is thick and fluffy. Pour into prepared crust. Chill for *at least* 2 hours. Can be frozen (leave out of freezer for 1/2 hour before serving).

Coconut Cream Pie

Preparation time: 15 minutes

Cool: 1 hour

Chill: 6 hours

Cooking time: 6 minutes (crust)

Serves: 6–8

6 oz. cream of coconut
1/4 cup milk
10 oz. mini marshmallows
3 cups heavy cream
1 cup flaked coconut
*1 10-inch baked pie shell
1 cup flaked coconut for top of pie

Mix 6 oz. cream of coconut with 1/4 cup milk in cooking pan. Add 10 oz. mini marshmallows. Cook over low heat until marshmallows melt. Cool in a large bowl and refrigerate for 1 hour or until mixture starts to gel. Beat gelled mixture, until frothy, with electric mixer. Carefully fold in 3 cups heavy cream that has been whipped stiff. Blend in 1 cup flaked coconut by hand. Pour into 10 inch baked pie shell. Sprinkle additional cup flaked coconut over pie and refrigerate at least 6 hours before serving.

Freezes beautifully.

*Pie shell may be purchased in supermarket (unbaked). Bake according to directions (bakes about 6 minutes).

Fudge Macaroon Pie

Preparation time: 10 minutes

Cooking time: 30 minutes

Serves: 6–8

3 squares Baker's unsweetened chocolate
1/2 cup butter or margarine
3 large eggs, slightly beaten
3/4 cup granulated sugar
1/2 cup all-purpose flour
1 teaspoon vanilla
2/3 cup sweetened condensed milk
2-2/3 cups flaked coconut

    Melt chocolate and butter in a saucepan over low heat. Stir in eggs, sugar, flour and vanilla. Pour into *greased* 9-inch pie plate. Combine milk and coconut. Spoon over chocolate mixture, leaving 1/2 to 1 inch border.
    Bake in preheated 350° oven for 30 minutes. Cool and serve.

German Sweet Chocolate Cream Pie

Preparation time: 10 minutes

Cooking time: 5 minutes

Freezing time: 4 hours

1 package (4 oz.) *Baker's German Sweet Chocolate*
1/3 cup milk
2 tablespoons granulated sugar
1 package (3 oz.) *cream cheese, softened*
3-1/2 cup (8 oz.) *non-dairy whipped topping, thawed*
8 inch graham cracker crumb crust

    Heat chocolate and 2 tablespoons of the milk in saucepan over low heat, stirring until chocolate is melted. Beat sugar into cream cheese; add remaining milk and chocolate mixture and beat until smooth. Fold in whipped topping, blending until smooth. Spoon into crust. Freeze until firm.

Macadamia Nut Pie

Preparation time: 20 minutes

Cooking time: 8–10 minutes

Refrigeration time: 2 hours plus overnight

Serves: 6–8

1 9-inch pie crust (baked)
1/2 cup granulated sugar
1/4 cup cornstarch
pinch of salt
3 extra large egg yolks
2 cups milk
1 tablespoon butter
1-1/2 cups heavy cream
2 tablespoons coffee liqueur
1/2 cup chopped Macadamia nuts
whole Macadamia nuts for garnish

Beat together granulated sugar, cornstarch, salt and egg yolks. Heat milk to the boiling point (but do *not* boil). Stir sugar mixture into hot milk. Cook for 5 minutes, stirring constantly. Remove from heat. Stir in butter. Cover with wax paper and refrigerate for 2 hours (or until mixture is cool). Beat 1/2 cup heavy cream and fold into cooled mixture with coffee liqueur and add all but one tablespoon of the chopped nuts. Pour mixture into pie crust. Chill in refrigerator overnight.

Whip remaining (1 cup) heavy cream. Spread over pie. Sprinkle remaining tablespoon chopped nuts over pie and garnish with whole nuts around edge.

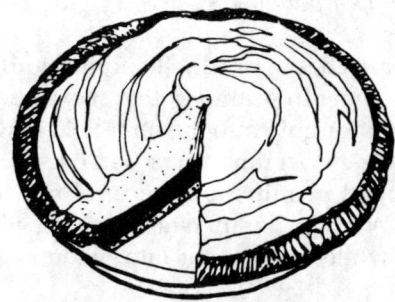

Peanut Butter Pie

Preparation time: 10 minutes

Freezing time: 4 hours or overnight

Serves: 6–8

4 oz. cream cheese, softened
1 cup confectioner's sugar
1 cup peanut butter
1/2 cup milk
8 oz. heavy cream, whipped or 1 package (9 oz.) non-dairy whipped topping
9 inch graham cracker crust, or cooked 9 inch pastry shell
1/4 cup chopped peanuts

Beat cream cheese until soft and fluffy. Beat confectioner's sugar in peanut butter. Slowly add milk, blending thoroughly into mixture. Fold in whipped cream. Pour into graham cracker crust. Sprinkle with chopped peanuts. Freeze until firm (at least 4 hours). Wrap in Saran Wrap after pie is frozen. To serve: while frozen, cut into medium to small pieces (return any remaining pie to freezer). Let cut pieces stand for at least 15–30 minutes before serving.

Quick Limeade Pie

Preparation time: 10 minutes

Refrigeration time: 2 hours or overnight

Serves: 6

1 can (14 oz.) sweetened condensed milk (not evaporated milk)
1 container (4-1/2 oz.) frozen non-dairy topping, thawed
1 can (6 oz.) frozen concentrate for limeade (thawed)
2 tablespoons fresh lime juice
3 drops green food coloring
1 prepared 8-inch graham cracker crust
lime slices

    Mix condensed milk into non-dairy topping in a medium-sized bowl. Stir in thawed limeade, lime juice and food coloring until well-blended.
    Pour mixture into graham cracker crust and refrigerate for several hours or until firm.
    Garnish with lime slices.

Strawberry Cream Pie

Preparation time: 15 minutes

Chilling time: 2 hours or overnight

Serves: 6–8

1 (8 oz.) package cream cheese, softened
1/4 cup granulated sugar
1/2 teaspoon vanilla
dash of nutmeg
1 cup of strawberry slices (fresh)
1 cup whipping cream
1/4 cup sifted confectioner's sugar
1 8 inch graham cracker crust

    Combine softened cream cheese, granulated sugar, vanilla and nutmeg, mixing until well blended. Mash 3/4 cup strawberries; add to cream cheese mixture. Add confectioner's sugar to heavy cream, beat until cream is whipped. Fold into cream cheese mixture. Pour into crust; chill several hours or overnight. Garnish with remaining strawberries.

Chocolate Apricot Viennese Cake

Preparation time: 10 minutes (cake)
  5 minutes (frosting)

Cooking time: 40–45 minutes (cake)
  5 minutes (frosting)

Serves: 8 to 10

Cake

1 can (16 oz.) Hershey chocolate syrup
1 cup all-purpose flour, unsifted
1 cup granulated sugar
1/4 teaspoon baking powder
1 stick (1/2 cup) sweet butter, softened
4 large eggs
1 teaspoon vanilla

Filling

Approximately 6 ounces of apricot preserves

Frosting

1-1/2 cup semi-sweet chocolate morsels
1/2 pint (4 ounces) commercially prepared sour cream
1/4 cup slivered almonds

Cake

Mix softened butter and all other ingredients together. Pour into one greased and floured 9 inch round cake pan. Bake in preheated 350° oven for 40 to 45 minutes. When cooled, slit cake in half, horizontally, and evenly spread one layer with apricot preserves.

Frosting

Mix chocolate bits and sour cream together. Melt over *low* heat.

Put plain layer of cake on top of layer that has been spread with apricot preserves.

Frost top and sides of cake.

Sprinkle top with slivered almonds (approximately 1/4 cup).

This is a very rich cake so serving slices should be fairly small. It is very chocolatey and not terribly sweet.

Jello Strawberry Cake

Preparation time: 10 minutes

Cooking time: 35 minutes

Freezing time: 1-1/2 hours

Serves: 8 to 10

1 yellow cake mix (18.5 oz.) (without pudding)
1-1/2 cups cold water
2 large eggs
2 tablespoons cooking oil
2 cups boiling water
2 (3 oz. each) packages strawberry Jello
8 oz. whipped topping
1/2 pint fresh crushed strawberries

Follow directions for making cake, but add 2 tablespoons cooking oil.

Bake in preheated 350° oven in 13" × 9" × 2" pan for 35 minutes.

Remove cake from oven and immediately prick holes in cake with meat fork all over.

Mix 2 cups of boiling water with 2 (3 oz.) packages strawberry Jello. Dissolve and pour over hot cake. Put cake in freezer for 1-1/2 hours. Run spatula around sides of pan and run hot water on bottom of pan to release cake to dish.

Cover the cake with small container of whipped topping to which half pint of fresh crushed strawberries have been added. Save a few strawberries for top of cake.

Refrigerate until ready to use.

Jewish Apple Cake

Preparation time: 15 minutes

Cooking time: 1-1/2 hours

Serves: 10–12

6 large apples, peeled and thinly sliced
3 tablespoons granulated sugar
3 teaspoons cinnamon
3 cups flour
2 cups granulated sugar
1 cup salad oil
4 large eggs
1/2 teaspoon salt
1/3 cup orange juice
2-1/2 teaspoons vanilla
3 teaspoons baking powder

Peel and thinly slice apples, sprinkle with mixture of 3 tablespoons sugar and 3 teaspoons cinnamon. Set aside. Combine all remaining ingredients, mixing well. Grease and flour a tube pan. Put in a layer of half of the batter, then a layer of 1/2 of the fruit and the remaining batter. Finish with a layer of apples. Bake in preheated 350° oven for 1-1/2 hours.

Desserts

Lemonade Cake

Preparation time: 10 minutes

Cooking time: 1 hour

Serves: 12

1 package (18-1/2 oz.) Lemon Supreme Cake Mix (without pudding added)
1 package (3 oz.) instant lemon pudding mix
4 large eggs
3/4 cup cooking oil
3/4 cup cold water
flour and margarine to grease pan
frozen lemonade (6 oz.), defrosted, not diluted
1/2 cup granulated sugar

    Combine cake mix, lemon pudding mix, 4 eggs, 3/4 cup salad oil and 3/4 cup cold water. Mix until smooth. Pour into a greased and floured tube pan. Bake in preheated 350° oven for 1 hour. Remove from oven and immediately pour defrosted lemonade that has been combined with 1/2 cup granulated sugar over cake. Prick cake with fork beforehand so lemonade permeates all. Let cake stand in pan until cool.

Rum Cake with Glaze

Preparation time: 15 minutes (total for cake & glaze)

Cooking time: 1 hour (cake)
                     7 minutes (glaze)

Serves: 12

Cake
1 cup chopped pecans or English walnuts
1 (18-1/2 oz.) package yellow cake mix
*1 (3-1/2 oz.) package Jello Vanilla Instant Pudding & Pie Filling
4 eggs
1/2 cup cold water
1/2 cup Wesson oil
1/2 cup Baccardi dark rum (80 proof)

Glaze

1/4 cup butter
1/4 cup water
1 cup granulated sugar
**1/2 cup Baccardi dark rum (*80 proof*)

Cake

Preheat oven 325°. Grease and flour 10-inch tube pan. Sprinkle nuts over bottom of pan. Mix all cake ingredients together. Pour batter over nuts. Bake 1 hour. Cool. Invert on serving plate. Prick top of cake with a fork. Spoon and brush glaze evenly over tops and sides. Repeat until glaze is used up.

Glaze

Melt butter in saucepan with low flame. Stir in water and sugar. Boil 5 minutes, stirring constantly. Remove from heat. Stir in rum.

*If using yellow cake mix with pudding already *in the mix*, omit instant pudding, use 3 eggs instead of 4, 1/3 cup oil instead of 1/2.
**Bourbon can be used in place of rum.

Strawberry Shortcut Cake

Preparation time: 10 minutes

Cooking time: 45 to 50 minutes

Serves: 10–12

1 cup miniature marshmallows
2 packages (10 oz. each) frozen sliced strawberries in syrup, completely thawed
1 package (3 oz.) strawberry-flavored gelatin
*2-1/4 cups all-purpose flour
1-1/2 cups granulated sugar
1/2 cup solid shortening
3 teaspoons baking powder
1/2 teaspoon salt
1 cup milk
1 teaspoon vanilla
3 large eggs

Generously grease the bottom *only* of a 13" × 9" × 2" baking pan; sprinkle marshmallows evenly over the bottom of pan. Thoroughly com-

Desserts

bine thawed strawberries and syrup with dry gelatin, set aside.

Combine flour (no need to sift) and remaining ingredients in large mixing bowl. Blend with mixer at low speed until moistened; beat 3 minutes at medium speed, scraping sides of bowl occasionally. Pour batter evenly over marshmallows in pan. Spoon strawberry mixture evenly over top of batter. Bake in preheated 350° oven for 45 to 50 minutes or until golden brown and toothpick inserted in center comes out clean.

Serve warm or cool with ice cream or whipped cream.

*Note: To use self-rising flour, omit *baking powder and salt.*

Cherries Jubilee

Preparation time: 5 minutes

Cooking time: 10 minutes

Serves: 6

1 quart vanilla ice cream
3/4 cup currant jelly
1 can (16 oz.) pitted dark sweet cherries, drained
1/4 cup rum
1 teaspoon grated orange peel
1/4 cup brandy

Melt jelly in saucepan over medium heat. Stir in cherries, rum and orange peel. Heat to simmering, stirring constantly. Heat brandy in small saucepan; slowly pour over cherries and ignite. Serve hot over ice cream.

Butterscotch Sauce

Preparation time: 5 minutes

Cooking time: 5 minutes

Serves: 12–14 (3-1/2 cups)

1/2 cup butter
1 cup heavy cream
1 (16 oz.) box dark brown sugar

Melt butter in saucepan over *low* heat. Stir in brown sugar and cream. Cook to boiling point. Remove from heat and cool slightly.

Serve over vanilla ice cream.

Chocolate Sauce

Preparation time: 15 minutes

Cooking time: same

Serves: 14 to 16 (makes 4 cups)

1/2 cup butter
4 (1 oz. each) *squares unsweetened chocolate*
3 cups granulated sugar
1 (13 oz.) *can evaporated milk*
1/2 teaspoon salt

Melt butter and chocolate in top of a double boiler (while water boils in bottom half of boiler); stir in remaining ingredients. Cook over medium heat stirring constantly until sugar is dissolved and sauce is smooth.

Serve hot or cold.

Fresh Fruit Cream Topping

Preparation time: 15 minutes

Cooking time: 10 minutes & refrigerate at least 2 hours

Serves: 8

1 envelope Knox gelatin + 1/2 cup of cold water
2 cups half & half
2 cups sour cream
1 cup granulated sugar
1 teaspoon vanilla extract

    Soften gelatin in 1/2 cup water—5 minutes. Combine sugar, half and half and gelatin in heavy saucepan. Heat to dissolve gelatin but do not boil, stirring constantly. Cool. Beat in sour cream and vanilla. Refrigerate and serve with any fresh fruit on top (strawberries, blueberries, green grapes, bananas, etc.).

Rum Sauce

Preparation time: 5 minutes

Cooking time: 5–8 minutes

Serves: 12–14 (3-1/2 cups)

2 cups water
1 cup granulated sugar
2 tablespoons (*heaping*) cornstarch
2 tablespoons butter
3–4 tablespoons rum (*more or less to taste*)

    In a saucepan, combine sugar and cornstarch. Add water, slowly, mixing well. Cook over low heat, stirring until mixture thickens. Remove from heat, add butter and rum.
    Serve warm over ice cream or cake.

Skillet Apple Dessert

Preparation time: 5 minutes

Cooking time: 5–7 minutes

Serves: 4

3 large red cooking apples
4 tablespoons butter or margarine
3 tablespoons light brown sugar
2 teaspoons lemon juice
3/4 teaspoon ground cinnamon
1/4 teaspoon salt
heavy or whipped cream (optional)

   About 15 minutes before serving: Core apples; cut into 1/2 inch-thick wedges (about the size of sliced canned peaches).
   In 12-inch skillet over medium heat, melt butter or margarine and add sugar, lemon juice, cinnamon and salt and cook apples in this mixture until they are tender, about 5–7 minutes. Stir and turn apples frequently. Spoon apples and their syrup into 4 dessert bowls. If you like, serve with heavy cream or put a dab of whipped cream on top.

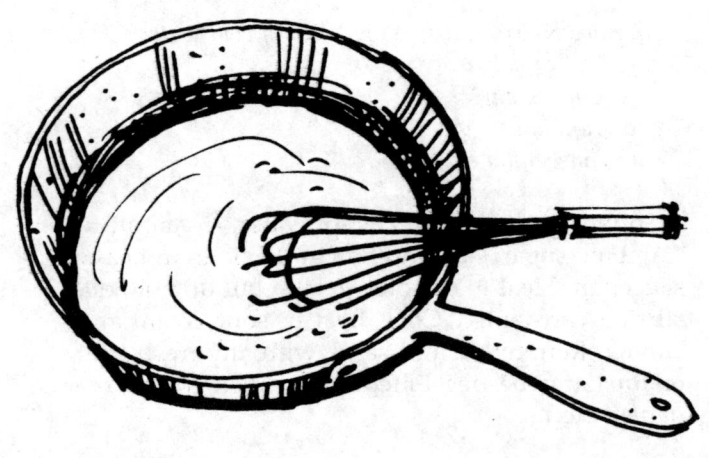

Bananas Foster

Preparation time: 15 minutes

Cooking time: 10 minutes

Serves: 2

2 tablespoons butter
4 tablespoons brown sugar
2 bananas
pinch of cinnamon
1 tablespoon banana liqueur
1 ounce rum or brandy
vanilla ice cream

Mix butter and brown sugar in saucepan. Cook over medium heat until it is carmelized (about 3 minutes). Cut bananas in quarters. Add to saucepan and cook until tender (about 4 to 5 minutes). Add cinnamon and liqueur; stir. Add rum or brandy to top of mixture. *Do not stir.* Ignite with match. Spoon over vanilla ice cream while flaming.

Easy Coconut Dessert

Preparation time: 5 minutes

Cooking time: 45 minutes

Serves: 6

2 cups milk
4 large eggs
3/4 cup granulated sugar
1/2 cup Bisquick
1/4 cup melted butter
1 teaspoon vanilla
1/2 cup flaked coconut

In an electric blender, at high speed, whisk together all the ingredients except the coconut, for 3 minutes. Turn into a buttered 9" × 1-1/4" pie plate; sprinkle with coconut; plate will be very full. Carefully place in a preheated 350° oven and bake until a knife inserted in center comes out clean—about 45 minutes. Serve warm or chilled.

Dessert Ice

Preparation time: 10 minutes

Cooking time: 0

Serves: 4–6

1 pint vanilla ice cream, slightly softened
1 pint pineapple sherbet
2 tablespoons Cointreau or Triple Sec
2 tablespoons Grand Marnier
1 teaspoon lemon rind, grated
1 teaspoon orange rind, grated

  Combine all and beat until smooth. Spoon into wine or champagne glasses and serve or put into freezer.

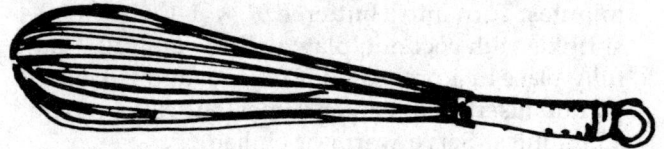

John's Favorite Strawberry Dessert

Preparation time: 25 minutes*

Cooking time: 20 minutes (crumb topping and bottom)

Freezing time: overnight

Serves: 8 to 10

Crust

1 cup all-purpose flour
1/2 cup chopped pecans or English walnuts
1/2 cup butter or margarine, melted
1/4 cup firmly packed brown sugar

Filling

1 (10 oz.) package frozen strawberries, thawed
1/2 cup granulated sugar
2 teaspoons fresh lemon juice
2 egg whites
1 cup whipping cream, whipped

Combine flour, chopped pecans or walnuts, melted butter and brown sugar in an 8-inch baking pan; stir well. Bake in preheated 350° oven for 20 minutes; stirring occasionally; cool. Combine sugar, lemon juice and egg whites in a large mixing bowl; beat at high speed of electric mixer 10 to 12 minutes or until stiff peaks form. Fold in thawed strawberries. Then fold whipped cream into all.

Press about two-thirds of crumb mixture into a 9-inch spring form pan or into 9" × 5" glass rectangular dish. Spoon in strawberry mixture. Sprinkle remaining crumbs on top. Freeze until firm (overnight).

This is a terrific recipe to serve to a large group; simply double quantity and freeze in 13" × 9" × 2" dish.

When serving, be sure to have dessert at room temperature for 15 or 20 minutes to soften somewhat before eating.

*Over usual 15 minute or less preparation time, but this is an easily prepared special dessert.

Baked Fudge

Preparation time: 10 minutes

Cooking time: 10 minutes

Chilling time: 1 hour

Serves: approximately 24 pieces

1 pound 10X powdered (confectioner's) sugar (4-1/2 cups)
1/4 cup milk
1/2 cup cocoa
1 stick (1/2 cup) butter
1 teaspoon vanilla
1 cup chopped pecans or walnuts (optional)

Mix all ingredients *except* vanilla and nuts together and place in a pyrex casserole. Bake in a preheated 350° oven for 10 minutes. Remove from oven; add 1 teaspoon vanilla and nuts and beat until firm (approximately 5 minutes). Pour into a greased 8" × 8" pan. Chill for approximately 1 hour.

Hello Dollys

Preparation time: 5 minutes

Cooking time: 25 minutes

Makes: 2 dozen

1/4 pound butter
1 cup graham cracker crumbs
1 12 oz. package semi-sweet chocolate chips
1 cup coarsely chopped English walnuts or pecans
1 8 oz. can sweetened condensed milk
1 3-1/2 oz. can flaked coconut

Preheat oven 350°.
Melt butter in 13" × 9" × 2" pan or pyrex dish. Sprinkle graham cracker crumbs over top of butter, then add coconut, then chocolate chips and then milk. Top with nuts and bake 20–25 minutes. Cool, then cut into 2-inch squares.

Pecan Brandy Pudding

Preparation time: 10 minutes

Cooking time: 45 minutes

Serves: 6 to 8

4 extra large eggs
1 cup granulated sugar
1-1/2 cups light corn syrup
1/3 cup melted butter
1-1/2 teaspoons vanilla
1/4 cup of brandy
1 cup finely chopped pecans

Combine all but nuts. Beat well. Stir in nuts. Pour into buttered 8" × 8" pan and bake in preheated 350° oven 45 minutes or until just set. Cool until just barely warm (about 12 minutes). Spoon into dessert dishes and add a scoop of vanilla ice cream.

Blueberry Cheesecake

Preparation time: 20 minutes

Cooking time: 35 minutes

Chilling time: overnight

Serves: 8

Crust

2 cups graham cracker crumbs
1/2 cup granulated sugar
2/3 cup melted butter

Cheese Filling

3 8 oz. packages cream cheese
1 cup granulated sugar
4 eggs
1-1/2 teaspoons lemon rind—grated rind of approximately 2 lemons (Also available in supermarkets already grated in jar)

Topping

1 pint blueberries
1 teaspoon grated lemon rind (rind of about one lemon)
1/4 cup water
1 teaspoon cornstarch mixed with 2 tablespoons water

Crust

Combine cracker crumbs, 1/2 cup sugar and butter and press over sides and bottom of 8-inch spring form pan.

Filling

Blend cream cheese, 1 cup sugar, eggs and 1-1/2 teaspoons lemon rind in electric blender or soften cheese and mix all ingredients until smooth.

Pour into graham cracker crust. Bake 35 minutes in preheated 350° oven. Cool and then refrigerate overnight. Then, add topping.

Topping

Combine blueberries, 1/4 cup water, 1 teaspoon grated lemon rind and 1 teaspoon cornstarch mixed with 2 tablespoons water in saucepan. Simmer for 1 minute. Cool. Pour over cream cheese filling. Refrigerate until serving.

Cheese Pie

Preparation time: 10 minutes

Cooking time: 35 minutes plus 45 minutes

Serves: 6–8

1 9-inch graham cracker crust
1 8 oz. package, plus 1 3 oz. package cream cheese, softened
1 cup granulated sugar
2 large eggs
1/2 pint commercially prepared sour cream
1 teaspoon vanilla

Cream sugar and cream cheese. Add remaining ingredients, mixing well and pour into graham cracker crust. Bake in preheated 350° oven for 35 minutes. Turn off oven and open oven door. Leave pie in oven for an additional 45 minutes to 1 hour.

World's Greatest Cheese Cake

Preparation time: 20 minutes

Cooking time: 40 minutes plus 5 minutes

Refrigeration time: overnight

Serves: 10–12

Crust

2 cups graham cracker crumbs (13 graham crackers)
5 tablespoons butter
1/4 cup granulated sugar
1 tablespoon vanilla

Filling

3 (8 oz. each) packages cream cheese, softened
1 cup granulated sugar
5 extra large eggs
2 teaspoons vanilla

Topping

1 pint commercial sour cream
4 tablespoons granulated sugar
1 teaspoon vanilla

Crust

Combine graham cracker crumbs, granulated sugar and vanilla. Melt butter over low flame and add to mixture. Press crumb mixture over bottom and sides of a spring form baking pan and refrigerate until filling is ready.

Filling

Soften cream cheese. Gradually add granulated sugar and beat thoroughly. Add eggs, one at a time, and vanilla, until blended. Pour into graham cracker crust and bake for 40 minutes in preheated 325° oven.

Topping

Mix ingredients (sour cream, granulated sugar and vanilla) well. Carefully spread on top of baked cheese cake. Bake for 5 minutes in 475° oven. Cool and refrigerate overnight.

Glossary

Glossary of Cooking Terms

BAKE   To cook by dry heat in an oven or oven-type appliance in a covered or uncovered container.

BARBECUE   To roast slowly on a spit or grid over slow-burning coals or under a broiler, usually basting with a highly seasoned sauce.

BASTE   To moisten (meat or other foods) while cooking to prevent drying and to add flavor. The liquid may be pan drippings, melted fat, butter, margarine, oil, fruit juice, sauce, or even salt water.

BEAT   To agitate with rapid, regular strokes that lift and turn the mixture, thereby incorporating air and making it smooth. The tool may be a spoon or wire whisk, a hand-operated rotary beater, or an electric beater of the air-incorporating type.

BLEND   To combine thoroughly two or more ingredients.

BOIL   To cook food in boiling liquid, usually water. A liquid is boiling when bubbles of its vapor continuously rise to the surface and break. The boiling temperature of pure water at sea level is 212°F. (100°C.).

BROIL   To cook directly under the heating unit or over an open fire.

BRUSH   To coat the surface with melted butter, oil, milk, cream, or beaten egg white, using a pastry brush.

CHOP   To cut into small pieces with a sharp knife.

COAT   To roll food in flour, crumbs, sugar, chopped nuts, etc., until uniformly covered; or to dip in bread crumbs, in egg and milk, and again in crumbs.

CREAM   To mix shortening until it is smooth and creamy by rubbing it against the side of the bowl with a spoon. This term is usually applied to mixing sugar with shortening in making a cake.

CUBE   To cut in small (1/2 inch square) pieces.

CUT   (a) To divide food into pieces with a knife or scissors.
   (b) To combine shortening with dry ingredients with two knives, a fork, or a pastry blender.

DICE   To cut into cubes 1/4 inch in size.

DOT   To scatter bits of butter, nuts, chocolate, etc., over the surface of food.

DREDGE   To coat with seasoned flour or other dry ingredients.

DRIPPINGS   Fat or juice that cooks out of meat or poultry and falls into the roasting pan.

DUST   To sprinkle or coat lightly with sugar or flour.

EGGS, LIGHTLY BEATEN   Beat only enough to blend yolks and whites.

EGGS, WELL BEATEN IN SOFT, STIFF PEAKS   Whites are beaten until stiff but not dry. They stand in moist, glossy peaks that droop over a bit when the beater is lifted from the eggs.

EGG WHITES, BEATEN VERY STIFF   Points of peaks stand upright without drooping when beater is removed. Surface should look dry.

EGG YOLKS, WELL BEATEN   Beat until yolks are thick and lemon-colored.

FILLET   Boneless strips of meat or fish.

FLAKE   To break into small pieces.

FLAMBÉ   To cover warm food with warmed brandy, rum, or liqueur of high alcohol content, to ignite and serve flaming (plum pudding, cherries jubilee).

FOLD   To combine ingredients by cutting vertically through the mixture and gently turning it under and over until thoroughly blended, using a rubber spatula, wire whip, or spoon.

FRY, SHALLOW FAT   To cook in a small amount of fat on top of stove. (Also called sauté or pan-fry.)

GARNISH   To decorate a dish with parsley, fruit slices, etc.

Glossary

GLAZE To make a smooth glossy surface by coating with a thin layer of aspic, melted jelly, sugar syrup, icing, or fruit juice sweetened and thickened with a little cornstarch.

GRATE To rub on a grater to produce fine particles.

JULIENNE To cut into thin strips.

MARINATE To let food stand several hours in a seasoned oil-acid mixture to improve flavor and tenderness.

MINCE To chop very fine.

PRECOOK To partially cook food in liquid below the boiling point.

PREHEAT To heat the oven to a given temperature before the food is inserted.

ROAST To cook by dry heat in an oven (see BAKE).

SAUTÉ To fry food in a small amount of fat.

SCORE To cut shallow gashes or slits in fat of meat before cooking (as in steaks) to prevent curling, or crisscross lines in ham before glazing.

SEAR To brown surface (of meat) over high heat or in very hot oven.

SIMMER To cook in liquid just below boiling point.

STEW To cook in a small quantity of liquid over gentle heat.

STOCK Liquid in which meat, poultry, fish, or vegetables have been cooked.

TOSS To mix with a light, quick motion without crushing or tearing the ingredients.

WHIP To beat rapidly to incorporate air and to increase volume, as in eggs, cream, and gelatin dishes.

Helpful Hints

To make soft cheese easier to grate:
Put cheese in freezer for 15 minutes

To make beef easier to slice in thin strips:
Put into freezer for an hour

To defrost meats quickly and safely:
Place in its original wrap (or foil) in a bowl of cold water to cover. Pour salt in water and on wrap. Cover with a lid and let stand for an hour.

To keep salt from clogging in shaker:
Add about 6 grains of rice to the shaker

To get skin off garlic before chopping:
Pound each clove with the side of a heavy knife

To hasten potatoes baking in regular oven:
Boil in salted water for 10 minutes before popping into a very hot oven

or

Insert a nail in potato—shortens baking time by 15 minutes

To ripen green bananas or tomatoes:
Wrap in a wet dish towel and place in a paper bag

To soften hard butter in a hurry:
Grate it

To remove cake from pan before it cools:
Turn cake upside down on a plate and rub ice cubes on the bottom of the cake pan

If a dish is too sweet:
Add a dash of vinegar

or

A dash of lemon juice

If a dish is too salty:
Add sugar

or

To soup or stew, add cut raw potato and discard once they're cooked and have absorbed the salt.

To prevent steaks from curling when you broil them:
Score the outer edges of fat with a sharp knife at 1-inch intervals

Sticky dates, raisins or figs will come apart easily:
If placed in your oven (350°) for a few minutes.

For a great-looking cake:
Frost first with a thin layer of icing. This will hold down crumbs and give an even base coat. When set or firm, the final frosting goes on easily and looks great.

Table of Equivalent Weight and Measures

Dash (liquid) = Few drops
Dash (dry) = less than 1/8 teaspoon
3 teaspoons = 1 tablespoon
4 tablespoons = 1/4 cup
5 tablespoons + 1 teaspoon = 1/3 cup
8 tablespoons = 1/2 cup
10 tablespoons + 2 teaspoons = 2/3 cup
12 tablespoons = 3/4 cup
16 tablespoons = 1 cup
2 cups = 1 pint
4 cups (2 pints) = 1 quart
4 quarts (liquid) = 1 gallon
8 quarts (dry) = 1 peck
4 pecks = 1 bushel
1 fluid ounce = 2 tablespoons
8 fluid ounces = 1 cup
32 fluid ounces = 1 quart
25 fluid ounces = 1 fifth (of gallon)

Substitutions

INSTEAD OF	USE	INSTEAD OF	USE
1 cup of fresh sweet milk	1/3 cup of instant non-fat dry milk plus 1 cup of water and 2½ teaspoons butter or margarine or 1/2 cup evaporated milk plus 1/2 cup of water	1 cup stock	1 bouillon cube dissolved in 8 ounces of hot water
		bread crumbs	rolled-out saltines
		flour, all purpose as a thickener	cornstarch
		garlic	garlic salt or garlic powder
1 cup of buttermilk or sour milk	1 teaspoon lemon juice or vinegar plus enough sweet milk to make 1 cup (let stand 5 minutes)	lemon juice	white sugar or lime juice or white wine
1 cup honey	3/4 cup sugar plus 1/4 cup of liquid		
1 square (1-ounce) unsweetened chocolate	3 tablespoons cocoa plus 1 tablespoon butter or margarine	mustard, prepared	powdered mustard
		scallions	green, plain or frozen onions or onion powder, to taste or 2/3 onion plus a garlic clove
2 egg yolks	1 whole egg		
1 medium size onion, chopped	1 tablespoon instant minced onion, dehydrated		

INDEX

APPETIZERS
Artichoke Spread	6
Baked Brie Pie	6
Bleu Cheese Bites	7
Bob's Favorite Corned Beef Spread	7
Cheese Ball	8
Cheese Puffs	8
Chutney Appetizer Spread	9
Crab Ring Appetizer	9
Hot Jezebel	10
Mystery Meatballs	10
Nachos	11
Nantucket Spread	11
Shrimp Mold I	12
Shrimp Mold II	12
Spinach Dip	13
Spinach Dip in Cabbage	14
Triscuit Topper	14

SOUPS
Corn and Tuna Bisque	15
Crabmeat Bisque	16
Crab Soup, Jenny's Favorite	17
Curried Pea Soup	16

BREADS
Aloha Muffins	18
Beer Bread, Easy	19
Cheese Bread	18
Cornbread	19
Garlic Bread	20
Zucchini Bread	20

SALAD DRESSINGS
Bleu Cheese Salad Dressing	34
Caesar Salad Dressing	35
Celery Seed Salad Dressing	35
Italian Salad Dressing	36
Pineapple Salad Dressing	36

SALADS
Apple-Bacon Salad	22
Caesar Salad	23
Cranberry-Pineapple Salad Mold	24
Curried Tuna and Apple Salad	24
Drew's Favorite Bleu Cheese Salad	25
Forgotten 4-Layer Salad	26
Fraser Cranberry Salad	26
Fresh Cauliflower Salad	27
Frozen Coleslaw	28

Index

Frozen Salad 28
Fruited Ham Salad 29
Golden Rice Salad 30
Greek Salad 30
Guacamole Salad 31
Ham and Melon Salad 32
Ham-Rice Toss 32
Hearty Ham Salad 33
Marinated Green Beans 33
Waldorf Salad 34

VEGETABLES AND SIDE DISHES
Broccoli Casserole 39
Broccoli/Cheese/Tomatoes 39

Corn, Creamy Italiano 41
Corn, Oven Barbecued 41
Corn Pudding 40

Eggplant Parmesan 42

Fruit, Baked with Sour Cream 47
Fruit, Hot Curried 48

Green Beans, Mediterranean 43
Green Beans Mushroom Combo 42

Peas, Continental 40

Potato, Herbed Baked 43
Potato, Irish Casserole 45

Rice, Seasoned Onion 44

Spinach Casserole 46

Squash, Texas Acorn 46

Tomatoes, Baked 38

CHICKEN/TURKEY
Apricot Chicken 50
Baked Chicken Reuben 50
Baked Orange Chicken 51
Chicken Breasts with Grapes 51
Chicken and Chipped Beef 52
Chicken Livers Supreme 53
Chicken in Wine 52
Curried Chicken 54
Hot Chicken Sandwich 54
Manhattan-Style Chicken (for grill) 55
Oriental Chicken 56
Oven-Fried Parmesan Chicken 56
Turkey or Chicken Casserole 57

SEAFOOD AND FISH
Crabmeat/Artichoke Casserole 61
Crabmeat Au Gratin 62
Crabmeat Mornay 63

Fish, Baked in Foil 58
Fish, Fillet of Flounder or Sole 59
Fish, Fillet of Sole Gourmet 59
Fish, Fillet of Sole with Sour Cream 60

Tuna Casserole ... 63
Tuna Topside Down Pie ... 64

CHEESE AND EGGS
   Chilies Rellenos Casserole ... 65
   Feather-Light Cheese Puff ... 66
   Impossible Quiche ... 66
   Skillet Cheese Toast ... 67
   Spinach Quiche ... 68
   Super Cream Sauce ... 69
   Welsh Rarebit ... 70

MEATS
   Beef Stroganoff ... 72
   Beef, Sweet and Sour ... 82
   Beefy Beans ... 73
   Brisket of Beef ... 73
   Brisket, Heavenly ... 77
   Chili and Corn Chips ... 74
   Cowboy Stew ... 75
   Cube Steak Italiano ... 74
   Flank Steak, Marinated ... 78
   Flank Steak, Terriyaki ... 82
   Ground Beef Skillet Dinner ... 76
   Hamburger with Cream-Cognac Sauce ... 76
   Meat Loaf ... 78
   Meat Loaf, Spicy ... 81
   Open-Face Reuben Sandwich ... 79
   Pizza Beef Pie ... 81
   Roast Beef, Perfect ... 80

   Ham, Curried and Peaches ... 84
   Lamb Steaks or Chops ... 83
   Pork Chops, Apple and Cabbage Skillet ... 87
   Pork Chops Cacciatore ... 87
   Pork Chops, Glazed Orange ... 84
   Pork Chops Hungarian ... 88
   Pork Chops, Maple Sauce (for grill) ... 85
   Pork Chops, One-Dish Meal ... 86
   Pork Roast, Orange Glazed ... 86
   Pork, Sweet and Sour ... 88

   Veal and Peppers Rosemary ... 89
   Veal and White Wine ... 89

SWEETS
   Baked Fudge ... 115

   Caramel Orange Ring ... 94
   Electric Skillet Coffee Cake ... 95

   Cheesecake, Blueberry ... 117
   Cheesecake, World's Greatest ... 119
   Cheese Pie ... 118

   Chocolate Apricot Viennese Cake ... 104
   Jello Strawberry Cake ... 105
   Jewish Apple Cake ... 106
   Lemonade Cake ... 107
   Rum Cake with Glaze ... 107
   Strawberry Shortcut Cake ... 108

Index

Hello Dollys..116

Bourbon Chocolate Chip Pecan Pie................. 96
Brickle Ice Cream Pie and Sauce 97
Chocolate Mousse Pie............................. 98
Coconut Cream Pie................................ 99
Fudge Macaroon Pie...............................100
German Sweet Chocolate Cream Pie.................100
Macadamia Nut Pie................................101
Peanut Butter Pie................................102
Quick Limeade Pie................................103
Strawberry Cream Pie.............................103

Butterscotch Sauce...............................110
Chocolate Sauce..................................110
Fresh Fruit Cream Topping........................111
Rum Sauce..111

Bananas Foster...................................113
Cherries Jubilee.................................109
Dessert Ice......................................114
Easy Coconut Dessert.............................113
John's Favorite Strawberry Dessert...............114
Pecan Brandy Pudding.............................116
Skillet Apple Dessert............................112